One Life to Live

by
Leigh Rhett

Bloomington, IN  Milton Keynes, UK

AuthorHouse™
1663 Liberty Drive, Suite 200
Bloomington, IN 47403
www.authorhouse.com
Phone: 1-800-839-8640

AuthorHouse™ UK Ltd.
500 Avebury Boulevard
Central Milton Keynes, MK9 2BE
www.authorhouse.co.uk
Phone: 08001974150

First published by AuthorHouse 7/18/2006

ISBN: 1-4184-0912-X (e)
ISBN: 1-4184-0913-8 (sc)
ISBN: 1-4184-0914-6 (dj)

Library of Congress Control Number: 2004092849

Printed in the United States of America
Bloomington, Indiana

This book is printed on acid-free paper.

Cover photography by the Author

If you would like to contact the author, please do so at azrhett@att.net

Prologue

Nothing new will be told here nor have I skill in the writing of books; therefore. I have done this work to hallow my own thoughts, not designing it for the welfare of others. By it the holy impulse within me to frame righteousness is strengthened; but, if a fellow creature should see it, my book will fulfill another end likewise.

-Shanti Deva

I have never studied so as to write a book, but I have done some study because I have written one, --not so as to shape my opinions but, long after they have taken shape, to help them, to back them up and to serve them.

...

I subsequently confirmed and strengthened them by other men's authority and by the sound reasonings of those ancients with whom I found myself in agreement...

-Michel de Montaigne

In reading and writing, you cannot lay down rules until you have learned to obey them. Much more so in life.

-Marcus Aurelius

Table of Contents

Chapter I

The Writer 1

The Night of Realization 2

Living Life 5

Chapter II

The Self 8

The Ego 15

Desire 27

Expectations 38

Attachment 42

Chapter III

Will, Choice, and Action 49

Honesty 57

Self-Discipline 61

Forgetting 65

Courtesy 66

Chapter IV

Marriage 69

Chapter V

The Meaning of Love 79

The Difficulties in Loving 84

Chapter VI

Pleasure 96

The Importance of Place 108

Chapter VII

The Rudiments of Health 113

The Ambiguities of Work.....................................117

The Problem of "Ought-Tos"................................122

The Clouds of Worry and Fear.............................126

Chapter VIII

Inborn Attitudes 133

Humor 135

Chapter IX

God and Worship 137

Chapter X

Conclusion 143

Afterword..147

Appendix

Words of Wisdom..151

Who is Who 170

Chapter I

The Writer

I am an elder and it is only as such that I write about living life. I am not a preacher or a teacher or a guru. Nor am I the best exemplar of the good life. But from my perspective, it seems to me that certain precepts, gained from experience and a perennial wisdom, offer us ample guidelines for living life well, guidelines largely self-evident and largely ignored. Too often, we live our lives wastefully and, in the end, regretfully. This is a shame. As human beings, we are capable of doing better. With understanding, common sense and reason, we can do better. We can live intentional, aware lives and fearless, content lives.

Happy lives. Realizing that we have one life to live, why not live it well?

* * *

The Night of Realization

The dreadful realization of one's own death must occur at some time in early life to everyone. I have never heard this moment of realization discussed by others and I have never asked another about it. My own children, when young, never asked me about it, which reminds me that I did ask my mother about death when I was very young. She said that death was life among the stars. I was completely satisfied.

I remember when later my own extinction came to me. I was a youth lying in bed one night, awake in the dark. The realization that I would cease to exist came to me as a profound shock. I lay there, my head buried in my pillow, trembling at the enormity of it, the inconceivable monstrosity of it, the unfairness of it. Appallingly, death means the end of the future.

Everyone must have experienced a similar episode and we all recover. The moment of truth fades; ordinary life insinuates our consciousness. Out in the darkness, automobile horns sound, lights glisten, and snatches of music drift in and out. In the morning, people make and drink coffee, go to school or work, gossip and fret, and wonder, "How am I doing?" People deceive a little now and then, complain a lot, and want a lot. They compete and compare, and they worry. For some, time hangs heavy. They are often bored and want only to have fun, all of this in the face of death, in the face of extinction.

But then, you say, what else can a person do? One cannot spend one's time morbidly contemplating death while keeping one's sanity. So we willingly, eagerly seek distraction. And the night of realization is pushed far into the background, but never completely out of mind.

All humans from the most primitive to the most civilized have fostered and nourished an illusion and myth to help them face death, other than by distracting themselves with entertainment and gossip. They have promulgated the obvious solution, a denial of death. There is an afterlife, a continuation of being for eternity. The problem with this delusion is its improbability. Every night each of us sinks into oblivion for a period of time, usually during our first sleep. We cannot say at what moment we went to sleep. Asleep, we cannot say to ourselves, "Now I am asleep." We have no memory of the time during which we were sleeping. In other words, we die during some portion of every night, yet deny permanent death as a possibility. It is hard for me to imagine how we all can sleep each night with a loss of consciousness and then suppose that when we die it will be different. I am aware of the argument that we dream and, therefore, have some sort of life during sleep, as distorted and fragmentary as dreams are. But is it conceivable that a dissolved organism can continue to dream? I think not.

Death, then, is extinction. There is no reprieve. It is not an event in the news or an event concerning only distant aunts and uncles. It is a certainty for each of us. I am emphasizing this not out of morbidity, but rather to drum home, so to speak, the fact that we have only one life to live and the consequent importance of living it well. Living it well is a possibility for each of us as a human being.

> *My business, my art, is to live my life.*
> *-- Michel de Montaigne*

* * *

Living Life

Faced with the inconceivable but relentless fact of our personal extinction, we need to figure out how to live life while we have it. Men and women have thought long and hard about living a good life and finding happiness or bliss in life. In my own words and for myself, I think that achieving a sense of well-being and contentment in life is a possibility and is sufficient for a good life.

To have a sense of well-being and contentment is to have no fear. No fear of others, of personal failure, of illness, of death. It is not the feeling of well-being and contentment that a good meal and drink induces, nor any other temporary state induced by a satisfied appetite. It is, rather, an overall and continuing state of calmness and acceptance, a state in which one is comfortable with one's self. The self is not a fortress where one defiantly takes a stand or a place where one cringes in self-absorption. It is rather the place in which one can flourish.

The kind of well-being and contentment I have in mind permits an openness and concern for others, because there is no fear of others. However, it does not preclude prudence. I am not thinking of a happy-go-lucky carelessness that usually hurts others, but rather the exercise of foresight and appropriate action within one's means and abilities. Those who experience well-being and contentment know what their means and capabilities are and accept them. They do not waste living time in fantasies and illusions beyond themselves or in pretense or in frustration about circumstances they cannot change. They live within their boundaries with satisfaction.

So humble a life? So limited in life? So undistinguished a life? Yes, indeed! With one life to live, it is my thought that if each day is to count, and at the end of the day or even in the middle of the day, we can say, "I am content with myself and with my life," we would be maximizing our living time.

Why are we all not living a life of well-being and contentment? Why, instead, are we more often living contentious lives with fear, anger and discouragement, lives of boredom and fatigue, as uncaring time, relentlessly, passes us by? Blindly, we look outside ourselves to others as our only clue for a better life, because we do not know the principles and guidelines for living a good life. We erroneously believe we can enhance our lives or, perhaps, escape our lives by immersion: immersion in the Great Sea of Externals. The more involved, the more absorbed we are in our work, entertainment, relationships, gossip and games, the more distracted we become. We abdicate control of our lives to external mandates, transferring responsibility for our lives to a perceived inevitability. "That's life," we say, with courage and resignation as we make the most of our fate, seeking occasional relief in parties and adventure travel. Meanwhile, we look outside ourselves to others who will show us the way, who also will cheer us along the way and who will reassure us and comfort us should we falter or have misgivings.

But in looking outside ourselves to others, we betray ourselves. We are looking the wrong way. The path to assurance, security, well-being, contentment and happiness in our one life experience will be found not outside but inside ourselves where we alone can change our lives.

Chapter II

The Self

When we look inside, what do we find? We find the self. Remarkable! Remarkable, because as humans we can, as a self, look at ourselves as though looking at an object other than ourselves. The self, of course, has no anatomical existence. We cannot transplant selves. Nor, for that matter, can we transplant souls. The soul is distinct from the self in my thinking, because the soul is usually endowed with immortality and with an ethereal holiness. Socrates believed in the everlasting soul. In contrast, the self is an entity intimately identified with our existence as a person, an entity we can talk to and do talk to. We frequently see people talking to their selves, often, older people who after many years, presumably, are on familiar terms with their selves.

If we can talk to the self, we can criticize the self, we can rebuke the self, we can monitor the self and with patience, persistence and encouragement, we can change the self. We can improve the self. However, the idea of the self as an entity that we can talk to raises a concept not familiar to everyone. Years ago, my son in college asked me to write something to help a friend recognize her self. I had the following thoughts to share:

The hardest part of a discussion of the self is to begin it. Most discussions of the self, which I know of, do not begin at the beginning. They mostly assume a pre-existent awareness of the self, the self as a concept. But if, instead, we have never before thought of the self as something to think about, as something to pay attention to, as something that can determine one's life, we will be frustrated by a discussion which assumes we have this awareness of the self. The problem, then, is how we introduce a self to the self.

One way, perhaps, is to remind ourselves of how self-aware we already are without giving it thought. How painfully self-aware we are. We ask and constantly wonder, "How am I doing?" "How do I look?" And we check the mirror in the bath, in the car, and in the store window to see how we look. What we really want to know is how we look to others. Since appearance is so important, we check our own appearance in the mirror, hoping to guess how others see us. Beyond the appearance, we also hope to be admired for our personality, which will portray us as attractive, likable, amusing, sexy, brilliant, and talented. That is a tough one. It is hard to buy personality at Macy's. But there are ways of developing a personality. The primary way is through imitation. We look for models and imitate them. If there are none at hand, we find them readily at the movies and on television. And so we study and practice the demeanor of our chosen model, the smile, the carry of the head, the hand gestures, the stance and also the language. We try to talk like our model. In a word, we develop and imitate personality.

There are other ways we try to answer the question, "How am I doing?" In school, we check our grades to find out. To find out what? To find out whether we are smart, whether we will get a job, and whether we are among the chosen or the doomed to mediocrity. Later in life, we check to see how we are doing by assessing our possessions, whether they are the latest, are stylish, are observed by others, and how they compare with the possessions of the others. Note that in all of this we are self-aware, that we pay lots of attention to ourselves. In fact, we often pay too much attention to ourselves, becoming hopelessly self-absorbed.

Have you ever seen a dog examining himself in the mirror, raising his muzzle, lowering his muzzle, baring his teeth, cocking his head to one side, then the other, and finally standing sideways for a full-length view? I have not and I suspect that you have not either. Think what this means. The dog does not know whether he looks ugly or handsome, fat or thin, old or young. He has no self-image. He is not aware he is a dog, not aware that he exists as a separate entity, an entity that is finite. But in all of our concerns about appearance, we humans exhibit self-awareness. We see ourselves in the mirror and know we are looking at ourselves. Away from the mirror, we carry in our heads a self-image, which we attempt to verify from time to time. And we can be enormously elated or depressed by enhancement of our self-image or diminution as we perceive it in the mirror that others present to us. Whether we have thought about it before or not, we all exhibit self-awareness and by our actions, we also demonstrate a unique human faith that we can change ourselves. Dogs do not apply lipstick.

We are now ready, perhaps, for a crucial step in our discussion of the self. If we can acknowledge what seems self-evident, that humans are self-aware and can make premeditated, self-conscious alterations in their external appearance, then we can be open to the suggestion that the same self-awareness would also allow us to make changes within ourselves. This is when life really becomes interesting. This is the realm within which humans can experience freedom, make choices, can grow, and find contentment. This interior world is also the world of the spiritual.

The interior world is much more difficult to comprehend than the external, because it is intangible. It consists of feelings, emotions, and thoughts. And how can we change these? Are they not simply reactions to the external stimuli of unpaid bills, no jobs, or rejection? "What do you expect me to do," you may ask, "feel happy because I am broke, have no job and see only hassle and humiliation in my life?" My answer might be a resounding, "Yes, you could be happy." But practically, I would answer, "No, not happy. Not now." One can, however, make a situation better than it seems at first. This can be done internally. It depends on one's perception. Perception, which is our interpretation of stimuli received by the sense organs, creates our world. This is to say that it is not the stimuli, but the perception of them that creates our reality. How we choose to see the world defines it.

A cliche of the therapeutic and New Age world is that adversity is an opportunity. I dislike this expression. When I think of the adversity in which most people live, it is offensive that those who are better off can smugly suggest that adversity is an opportunity. And yet, there is some truth to it. I have always been impressed by the sight of apparently happy peasant women scrubbing their laundry on hands and knees by a Mexican stream. The argument was, also, made by the Stoics that one can be happy even as one is being tortured. I suspect, however, this is a theoretical assertion. But the point is that human beings can alter their lives so much internally that the external world becomes irrelevant. Mirrors are discarded.

I am not interested here in the heroics of human life. Not interested yet, although true heroics, I believe, are achieved internally. For now, we are discussing the notion that there exists an inner self. It is there within us that our lives can be changed. We can experience lived lives, rather than simply living life.

Turning inward, becoming aware of our inner life, our emotions, feelings, and thoughts is often called finding oneself. This is a self to which a discussion of the self usually refers, not the body self, the appearance, apparel, and conduct of which we are very aware. The ability to be aware of the inner self, to change it, control it, even suppress it (as paradoxical as that may sound) requires vigilance and a constant reminder to ourselves of ourselves. The temptation not to live our lives, but to live others' lives through gossip, news, speculation, theatricals, and games is overwhelming. How to regain ourselves, how to live ourselves is a subject of religious, as well as therapeutic, thought. But fundamentally it requires an awareness of the self and mindfulness.

This was my response to my son. I have no idea whether it made any impression. However, I was duly thanked for my effort.

We can improve the self. The self is not a prisoner of external circumstance, nor entirely an accident of birth. However, changing the self, especially improving it, is no easy task. There is an aspect of the self that can distort, deform and blight one's life. That characteristic of the self is the ego.

* * *

The Ego

The ego as an aspect of the self is, like the self, a figment of our imaginations. We cannot locate the ego in our anatomy. However, it is a useful concept in describing those actions and thoughts that promote, assert, and defend ourselves. The ego compares itself with others. The ego seeks to surpass others. It demands confirmation from others and it needs to control and dominate others. The ego asserts our individuality against others.

As separate individuals with egos, we continuously compare ourselves with other individuals. We not only compare ourselves to others, we speculate about how others see us. It is, perhaps, this speculation about the thoughts of others that dominates our lives. We are guessing all the time how others evaluate us. We are alert to clues of recognition and affirmation. We determine our worth by how we perceive that others perceive us, and our lives are spent in bolstering our worth by showing off our goods and asserting our rights. We are absorbed by the impression we hope to make on others. What that impression is, is our own self-image, a purely imaginary picture of ourselves that we hope to project.

The ego is ever vigilant and unrelenting in promoting its self. The ego often is fists up, challenging, assertive and combative in its role. It consequently creates tension and anger while also creating vulnerability to defeat and hurt. Its actions are not conducive to one's well-being. Obviously, the ego needs to be diminished, but how does one diminish one's ego?

One thing we can do to diminish the ego is to remind ourselves of our personal vulnerability and frailty. Consider the fact that our living experience depends upon a vehicle which functions without our saying so. We do not consciously extend or contract the heart, nor do we consciously breathe each breath. We do not digest our food knowingly. In fact, we do not control these automatic functions of our bodies and yet our existence depends on them. We exist only with the automatic functioning of our body.

To dramatize our plight, imagine that we are integral parts of our automobile. We are attached by the feet to the brake and the accelerator and by the hands to the steering wheel. When the car is new we are sleek and powerful and pretty and daring. After a few years, however, we notice newer cars around us stealing attention.

There are some dents in our body and we begin having some bad luck. We get a flat tire. It happened in the driveway. Not a big problem. But at the garage we are advised that all four tires are worn and need replacement. Four new tires take a large chunk out of savings. We have no insurance to cover tires. Then worse luck, our shock absorbers give out and need replacement. Other small replacements follow over the years, parking light bulbs, windshield wiper blades, some engine hoses and such. But the car functions satisfactorily, although no longer an eye-catcher.

Reconciled as we are to our present state, we are not prepared for what happens next. One day the automatic transmission fails and we discover that we will need to have the old transmission removed and a new one put in. This is a catastrophic event for us because of the time lost while in the garage and the cost of the new transmission.

In fact, the transmission operation is a shattering experience. Think of its implications. Major components are now requiring replacement. The car cannot be rebuilt piece by piece with new parts. Neither can we buy another. We are inseparable from this one. We feel exactly as we felt in the new car many years ago. Nothing has changed within ourselves. It's just the car that is disintegrating. We realize now, we really know now, that when the car gives out, our existence ends. We have known all along that other automobiles get old and finally die. But somehow that did not affect us until now, until our own transmission gave out. Why? Why should our existence be determined by a deteriorating machine? We can prolong its usefulness by care and good maintenance, but we can never change the outcome. It will inevitably disintegrate and disappear and our self with it.

And so when the transmission gives out we wonder what was all the sound and fury about, the ambition, disappointment, envy, jealousy, and fear that preoccupied us in the past? What difference did any of it make when eventually the car body slowly disintegrates? Ought we not have spent our days in better ways?

While it is deflating to the ego to realize how helpless it is in protecting and promoting the self when the self is predestined to extinction, it is equally deflating to realize how insignificant the self is in a historical or global sense. Look at an old black-and-white photograph of a crowd of people taken, say, fifty years ago. The men are all in suits and straw hats and the women with bobbed hair in bobby socks and saddle shoes. How strange they appear, yet look at the faces, the young faces, some flirtatious, some arrogant, some innocent, all self-conscious and all immortal, exactly like today's young faces. Then ask, how many of these faces are living today? Also, one might reflect that no dog, bird, or other small animal, alive on the planet then, lives today. As you look at the picture fifty years after it was taken, you may feel great sadness for the self-absorption and self-importance revealed in those young faces as though they had, over time, any importance at all. How many of us, today, know our grandparents' names?

That is not all. The truth is that the ego, a fiction, inhabits a fictitious realm. We live in an imaginary world created in our minds, absorbed by imagining the thoughts, motives, intentions and judgments of others, often as they relate directly or indirectly to ourselves. And on the basis of these imaginings, we mold our own actions, create our own aspirations, and our own fears. We spend endless hours of our one life speculating about what others are thinking. As a matter of fact, I suspect the greater part of our lives is spent in this futile occupation. Still, nearly all of us are doing it. One can imagine a vast network of crisscrossing mental speculations into which we are all hooked and in which we live our lives, a phantom existence with no meaning, no substance, no relevance to our being. Can you imagine any other animal on the planet living its life out in such a crushing mind web? I am not suggesting that we could or ought to live like animals. To the contrary, I might ask why we as intelligent human beings choose to live fictitious lives. From my perspective, it is folly--a waste of life.

For a self-aware person who realizes how transitory and brief life is, how common and ordinary the phenomena of birth and death are, the insistent work of the ego becomes an exercise in futility. For such a person the ego is unnecessary baggage to be unloaded as soon as possible. Remembering who we really are helps us to unload.

At this point I wish to digress with the observation that only we as humans can foresee our preordained fate. My assumption is that other animals do not foresee death even at the moment of death. Animals, therefore, do not fear death, and do not seek immortality. But we wish to perpetuate the self and we believe ourselves immortal, giving ourselves an importance we do not usually attribute to other animals. Few of us believe that the chicken sandwich we just consumed for lunch was the body of an immortal soul. But on what grounds do we make this distinction? Our behavior, if witnessed by an intelligence in outer space, could hardly be seen as distinct from other animal behavior except that we kill each other for no apparent purpose. Other animals kill animals of a different species for food. We kill our own species and do not eat the victims. We also kill almost every other species and we do eat those victims. We kill other lives just like all other animals, except we cook our dinner before consuming it and drink a glass of wine with it. To an intelligence watching the world from outer space, our bodies and our behavior are fundamentally no different from those of other animals. I have been told, whether true or not I do not know, that the entrails of a pig are almost indistinguishable from those of a human. And what about our fundamental behavior? Our observer from outer space would find uniformity among all animals, including humans in their dominant behavior patterns: the procurement of food, consumption of food, defecation and procreation. With regard to procreation our observer would notice a difference between the human species and other species. Humans are constantly involved in sexual activities, whereas other animals are only periodically involved when the female is biologically receptive. For humans, sexual interest is continuous and consuming.

It would not be unreasonable for the outer-space observer to conclude that the meaning of all the ceaseless activity he has observed on this planet is the production of fertilizer. He has noted with interest that life on earth is self-sustaining. Its purpose, apparently, is to provide fertilizer for the renewal of life. If our observer's view is distressing to ourselves, it behooves us to ask in what way it is wrong--what has he missed?

He has not missed our marvelous inventions or our understanding of the physical world. He is not deceived by our household appliances, computers, nuclear explosions or flush toilets. None of these technologies have changed our basic animal patterns of behavior. He has noted human distinctions in killing and copulating, but sees them as aberrations in animal behavior. However, I believe he has missed one form of human behavior that is truly distinct. Despite all the gluttony, wantonness, and carnage that human behavior produces, there is one act that is radically different from other animals. This is the act of self-denial. Standing aside and allowing another to pass is an expression of humanity.

> *A human being's most powerful act is*
> *willing renunciation of self-interest.*
> *-- Chandogtya Upanishad*

Returning now to the ego, self-denial aborts the ego and with it desire. I am not talking about self-denial as martyrdom. Again, we get hung up on what others will think of us. Self-denial, because others will praise or admire us, is not self-denial that thwarts the ego, but rather a strategy of the ego. The self-denial I have in mind is in action rather than words. It does not announce itself, nor does it accept praise. It is a self-denial that is comfortable, that earns its own reward regardless of recognition by others. It is internal, natural, personal and life-enhancing. It is a private matter within ourselves. It begins, I believe, with small denials that limit excesses of appetite, self-assertion and accumulation. Such self-denial dismantles the ego structure, quenches desire and opens the ground for a peaceful living experience

One might ask, however, since we are all fated to the same inevitable end, why not take as much advantage as one is able to take over others, and the environment, to make one's own predestined life more comfortable and enjoyable? In other words, the ego's work is justified. Such a position is rationalized by the free-market economy where personal aggrandizement is a virtue. The independent moneymaker is driven by self-interest and self-aggrandizement. Acquisitiveness and competitiveness are venerated in such an environment. Ego needs are intense. And in such a society based upon the glorification of the individual and his rights, it is especially difficult for one to turn about and attempt to repress one's ego. Despite the difficulty, it is nevertheless essential, if one is to experience well-being and contentment in one's life.

Let's look back at the inevitability and discomfort which an ego-self will experience, which compares itself always with others, which seeks to surpass others, which needs confirmation from others, and which needs to control and dominate others. That discomfort can never be eased or healed as long as the ego consumes our self-consciousness. No matter how much one achieves, there will always be others to be envied, to be controlled, others who fail to notice and applaud, others who disappoint and challenge, others who excel and surpass oneself. It is, of course, a matter of perception, lived out in that mental mesh of speculation about the thoughts of others. The point is that, to extract oneself from that web, we need, I think, to diminish the ego and seek selflessness.

This is not a moral imperative. It is a commonsense, practical choice for promoting one's well-being, just as running a mile each day is also a choice for well-being. It is, I believe, undeniable that fear and anger are reactions to a perceived threat to oneself, and fear and anger are not the ingredients of contentment and well-being. They are the ingredients for stress, which is distressful, since the dis-ease caused by stress is usually unreal. The perceived threat exists in our world of speculation and is rarely, for humans, an actual threat to survival. The problem is one of pride and face, and an exaggerated self-importance. Selfless, there would be no cause for fear and anger. Logically then, we ought to become selfless to avoid the agony of envy, jealousy, inferiority, hurt and despair. I have said this is a practical matter, not a moral imperative. But also as a practical matter, I know none of us will become completely selfless. The point is that each step toward selflessness will pay off in a release of tensions and a momentary, if not permanent, contentment and well-being. By diminishing self-importance we diminish the self-ego.

At this point, it might be helpful, to me at least, to retrace my thoughts in my rambling discourse so far. I began by expressing my thoughts about the monstrous reality of our own extinction. I hoped to convey that we, each of us, our own selves, are the subjects of death. We, unlike other animals when the cards were dealt, received the capacity to know our own end, not just at the moment of capture by a predator, but rather in safety and good health. Coupled with this knowledge, humans were also dealt an enormous brain and an intelligence commensurate with it. With intelligence, we can live deliberately, unlike other animals. With good reason, we can live a good life.

Good reason understands cause and effect. It understands that certain behaviors and certain attitudes lead to certain results. Being animalistic, demonstrating thoughtless behavior and grabbing every advantage for oneself, results in alienation, anxiety, and fear to a magnified extent among humans, since humans can project themselves into the minds of others. Thus, beyond the simple law of survival of the fittest, which among animals is played out on the physical plane, humans elevate the whole process to an ephemeral, nonphysical, mental plane of speculation that never ends. Thus, for humans, the good life is not found in instant gratification or death. It is complicated by imagination, speculation, and imputation. Yet again, with human intelligence, the possibility also exists to deliberately, thoughtfully and insightfully control one's reactions to the human environment.

* * *

Desire

Desire, like ego, is also an aspect of the self and is often responsive to our ego needs. However, not all desire is deleterious. We can desire the well-being of another or the success of some undertaking in the general interest of others and we can feel good about it, until and unless we develop an inordinate attachment to the desired outcome. In that case, if the desired outcome is not forthcoming, we have subjected ourselves to bitter disappointment and even anger. These emotions are not components of equanimity or peacefulness. We may also desire to be a good person, truthful, dependable, well-wishing and agreeable. This desire provides beneficial motivation worthy of cultivation. It is not an undesirable desire.

Another category, altogether, is desire arising from want. One who is wanting is usually one who is experiencing deprivation, a lack of something--for example, food, a tool, information or assistance. Severe want can impede well-being and the capacity for well-wishing toward others because of its self-interest in survival, but this is not necessarily the case. Examples of those who share with others, despite critical personal want, are common. Want is an external happenstance.

It is not a chronic disposition of the self. It is ordinarily justifiable desire beyond one's control.

The desires for personal growth, the well-being of others, and relief from deprivation are relatively benign. In contrast, other desires are deadly. They are life-destroying. Foremost is craving. Craving is physiological desire. It is appetite. It demands sensory satisfaction, which can be satiated only momentarily. Inevitability, sensory titillation wanes. Hunger returns. Often in desperation we strive to recapture the taste, the thrill or the intoxication of a previous high and our repeated desires end in addictions to sugar, chocolate, caffeine, nicotine, alcohol, and other drugs, not to mention superfluous quantities of unwholesome food. Addicted, our lives are in bondage. We become slaves to our appetite; we are out of control of ourselves. We are miserable.

Appetite in excess is invariably harmful to our bodies. I believe that whenever we do damage to our bodies or neglect the needs of our bodies, we become depressed. We have a constant low-grade case of guilt. We neither recognize the guilt nor the cause, but depressed and guilty, we can have no sense of well-being and contentment. In fact, depressed, we cannot change ourselves, but instead, sink deeper into the morass of desire grown stale. We carelessly waste our way into decay and disintegration, hoping or pretending that our desires are as intense as ever when in fact they are killing us. If one's eyes were as educated as a doctor's must be, then aging is not what it seems to be. Overweight, clogged arteries, potbellies, stooped shoulders, weak legs are not natural aging phenomena. There is, obviously, an aging process. But what we accept as aging is not aging. It is self-destruction.

There is no secret about living a healthy and vigorous life well into one's 90s. Scott Nearing, among others, showed us how. He died in his 100th year at his own choice in his own home, well, not sick. He chose to fast. After six weeks he died peacefully with his wife of 53 years beside him.

Scott and his wife, Helen, lived first in Vermont and then in Maine on farms and in homes they had built or remodeled themselves. They were self-sufficient in food and shelter. Moreover, this lifestyle was one designed by themselves, not something imposed by circumstance. According to Helen Nearing, Scott showed no physical weakness before the age of 90.

You may not wish to live to be 100, or so you say now, or live on a farm in New England. But I am suggesting that, if you want to know how to live a long and healthy life, there is no secret about it. The Nearings reduced their desires to a minimum, provided for themselves their food and shelter and apparently lived with great satisfaction and awareness. They wrote about it at length.

My argument then is that desire is insatiable and is harmful, as well, to our body and mind. Realizing this, looking at the price of one's own desire in a mirror, a thoughtful person will want to change course. This cannot be done with a New Year's vow.

Vows are unnecessary. Vows are, usually, a kind of oath, publicly declared. It is their publicity that elicits compliance. Lacking personal conviction, one takes a vow to fortify a weak resolve. Breaking a vow involves loss of face and so breaking a vow usually begins in secret. And most vows are broken.

Unless one has come to deplore or despise a habit or craving, one will not overcome it by publicly vowing to overcome it. The decision must be a private and determined one, often driven by fear of the consequences of a bad habit or addiction. Success depends upon truly valuing one's only life and, consequently, the need to preserve and enhance it. This cannot be accomplished with a vow.

How, then, can we begin to control our desires--our appetites?

I am a gradualist. When we are offered a new exotic food we usually take a very small first taste, and then, perhaps, another and another until we find how good it is. Snake is eaten in China and Mexico and, perhaps, in many other countries. It is said to taste like chicken, only better. If you are an American, urged and encouraged to eat snake, you probably won't take a vow to become a snake eater. Instead, you will take a small first bite. I urge the same approach in quenching desire. I realize this does not work well as an analogy, because getting to like snake meat develops a desire, while our goal is the quenching of desire. Still, it is amusing to think that the way we would cultivate a desire for snake meat is the same way we would quench our desire for ice cream, by saying no to a second helping and then, gradually, saying no to any helping at all. We would quickly find that the second helping, and then the first helping, are not missed and we feel better physically and, especially, psychologically. We are proud of our determination and proud of being in control of ourselves.

In warning, though, let me point out that one pitfall still exists. Having discovered our strength to control our desire, we now feel free to indulge again, convinced that we should stop whenever we want. The record will tell. Did we really stop or only suspend? I am talking about snake meat and ice cream, not cocaine or heroin, substances that cause physiological dependence. In these cases, it sounds naive to advise addicts to just say no in small steps.

Perhaps at bottom that is the answer, but it is not a simple answer. It is a very difficult answer. And before there are rewards there is pain and agony and often a need for help. However, as I said earlier, I am not addressing dire and extreme cases of personal degradation; rather, I have been discussing ways we, who are attempting with reason to improve the quality of our one living experience, can succeed.

It will be helpful, I believe, to look at desire in several categories. The dictionary offers the following synonyms for desire: wish, want, crave and covet. These synonyms suggest the categories of desire that might be useful in thinking about desire, remembering always that mental constructs are never airtight compartments and that the borders are blurred and interwoven. It is a common temptation for the critic to point out triumphantly that he has found elements of other categories within a category, or inconsistencies in the invariable application of a category. This revelation does not destroy the usefulness of the concept when it is remembered that categories display general tendencies and nothing more. So it is with wish, want, crave and covet. They are interwoven but useful.

To wish for something is a mild expression of a desire to have something occur which you think is improbable, but which you wish would happen. This is not an impediment to our well-being, unless, as I pointed out earlier, we become emotionally attached to the outcome.

To want, as discussed above, is an expression of a desire to have a need met. It is, usually, circumstantial and not a habit of the heart.

To crave is desire of appetite and sensuality. It is never satisfied except momentarily. It is the cause of disability and discontent. It is driven by physiological need, but is not necessarily always addictive. For instance, it was reported that women more than men crave chocolate and that men more than women crave meat. Both of these cravings may be injurious to health in the long run. However, the consumption of both chocolate and meat can be reduced or abandoned, quite easily. On the other hand, the craving for substances that alter consciousness can lead to addiction and misery. As we have seen, they can be fateful.

To covet is envious desire. It is desire for what others have. Obviously, to covet is the desire most opposed to well-being and contentment. It is secret desire, gnawing away at one's innermost self and causing discontent and ill will within oneself.

Covertness arises out of the ego. As we diminish the ego, we will banish covertness.

There are other desires arising largely out of the ego. Among them are intangible desires such as the desire for recognition, acceptance, inclusion and control. These are largely imaginary desires, imaginary in the sense that we imagine ourselves, for example, as having higher economic and social status and, often, we desire this status passionately. We are consumed by it. It is called ambition and is generally applauded. It is in fact a sad desire. Like other desires, it is never satisfied. Each step on a fictitious ladder leads to another higher step. Each step achieved is savored only momentarily. Then, one confronts oneself again with the same old ego, demanding even more. Like travel to far places, we carry with us up the ladder of success our flawed selves. Relying on externals and superficialities to improve our lives is, again, human folly.

In seeking higher status, a figment of the imagination, we think not of its responsibilities but rather the material manifestations of it: the accoutrements, accessories and symbols of it. Our worth is, in our minds, measured by appearances. By transference we assume that our worth in the minds of others is established by our possessions. We, therefore, desire desperately success symbols, gas-guzzling sport-utility vehicles for cross-country adventure, large homes with five bathrooms (just in case), entrances adorned by columned porticoes, swimming pools and Doberman pinschers. So desperately are these symbols desired, we often borrow them to put up a pretense of ownership, submitting our living experience to the tyranny of lenders. Even if we can buy outright the symbols of our worth, they in no way assure us of our happiness. We can drive only one car at a time and sleep in only one bed at a time no matter how many we own. Asleep, we experience the same dreams and nightmares as always and nature's calls as often, reminding us that wealth liberates us from poverty, but not from ourselves. Mother Teresa observed as much poverty in New York City as in Calcutta, poverty of the soul.

In summary, desire is largely an expression of ego. We desire something to have or to happen. We desire it badly, sometimes obsessively. It consumes our every thought. We desire a new BMW convertible, we long for a phone call from a certain person, or we yearn for a job promotion. Our very lives depend on it, most of all our self-image, who we are. Let's assume all our desires are fulfilled. It is inevitable in the experience of mankind that, once our desires are fulfilled, new desires arise. Desiring, we are never satisfied; craving, we are never satisfied. Momentary satisfaction or relief there may be, but only that.

To the intelligent person it must occur that it is not the external world doing us in, but rather our own desire for the exterior world. Consequently, we need to curtail our desires. Desire and ego go hand in hand. Why do we want the things we want so much? Are they essential to survival? I mean physical survival, not self-image survival. Nine times out of ten they are not. What we are so concerned about is appearances, what we think others will think of us, which is irrelevant to our onetime existence on this earth. We have to keep remembering that.

There is a tremendous difference between desire and need. When we can make the distinction in complete honesty, we can start eliminating and extinguishing most of our desires. Then, by clear thinking, we will have relieved ourselves of unnecessary disappointment, frustration and envy, all of which gnaw away at our being, clouding and distracting our attention from our reality--one life, one opportunity to live well. There is no second chance.

It is not, however, only material desires that plague us. We are obsessed equally by desires for fame, notoriety, or simple recognition. We want to be within the herd and within it, approved of, applauded, well-known, well-liked, and admired. Desiring this, we carefully observe those behaviors, mannerisms, enthusiasms, attitudes, and preferences of others that seem to have approval. We emulate them, because we desire acceptance and approval. But since many of these modes do not reflect our own nature, they are unnatural and untrue. Pretending to be something one thinks one ought to be would be like wearing misfit armor. It is painful. Role-playing is a waste of one's life.

We often believe that not playing the game will make us a maverick and an oddball. Unfortunately, there are some, especially among the young, who feel that not playing the game requires playing another game, which suggests that they are not over their desire for attention, recognition and acceptance. Playing a different game will prove to be equally a waste of life. To be oneself and live one's life as an aware and intelligent human being requires no statement. It can be done simply, genuinely, honestly and unobtrusively, anywhere, anytime, anyplace. Incidentally, it also does not require any vows, rituals, memberships or faith commitments. It only requires intelligence and reality consciousness. In legal jargon, it requires what a reasonable and prudent person would do.

And so, without further demonstration, I think that the case can be made that the ego and its accompanying desire infect our lives with discontent. Having one life to live, we cannot afford to spoil it in the coils of thoughtless hunger and aspiration. Intelligence suggests that we diminish our ego and our desire. I have said diminish, not eradicate. I propose the possible, not the impossible.

* * *

Expectations

There is a habit of thought we all share, which is more often harmful than useful. I have in mind our expectations. Expectations anticipate future events in the exterior world but are created within ourselves. We have expectations for occurrences and for behaviors by others. We become disillusioned, disappointed and angry when our expectations are not met, and when they are not, we begin at once to find and assign blame. We also seek to gain control: control to force people and events to meet our expectations. But control is conflictive. Gaining control is adversative. Having control, a headache. It is doomed, because one cannot control unforeseen events and unforeseen behavior by others. Worse yet, we often fail to meet our own expectations for ourselves.

Our intelligence tells us, then, to abandon all expectations. The world is not obligated to meet our expectations. On the other hand, the exterior world has no intent to frustrate our expectations, and no awareness of having done so. The best we can do to achieve peace of mind is to be an active participant in the world with no expectations regarding outcomes, certainly not outcomes that depend on others. Some mechanical devices have a reasonable probability of meeting expectations, but that simply magnifies the disappointment and discontent when they fail. Again, our best resort is to have no expectations.

He is not surprised because he is not disappointed, and he escapes disappointment because he never forms any expectations.
-- Samuel Johnson

I realize that I have been discussing expectations of future outcomes that are favorable. What about expectations for unfavorable outcomes? Expectations for the worst? Are they not insurance against future disappointment? Do not such expectations allow us to prepare in advance to minimize harmful outcomes? I must confess that this is my habitual attitude, protecting myself against future disappointment and loss. But there is a price. In the present, I am fearful, I am worried, I am preoccupied, and I am distracted. The quality of my onetime life experience has been forfeited to an often exaggerated, always imaginary future outcome. The anticipated eventuality will never in detail be anything like I imagined it to be. I am thinking mostly of outcomes expected in the realm of human affairs. On the other hand, it would be folly on a warm October day not to begin bringing in the wood for an expected cold winter day. It would be even greater folly to have an expectation that someone else would come along and bring the wood in for me.

Diminishing our ego, desires, and expectations is made possible when we reflect upon the reality of our existence. In that reality, our planet has existed for millions of years, not thousands, not hundreds, but millions of years. Life has existed on the Earth for large part of that time. Life is a continuum, while individual life is not. The geese on the pond each winter are the same. The individual geese are not.

The purpose of individual life may be simply to reproduce itself so that life continues. From this perspective, the momentary flame, which is an individual life, is insignificant. It is insignificant in the overall scheme. And it is well that we remember this when the consequences of our daily life seemed to us so important. One of the greatest assists to our effort to contain our ego, desires, and expectations, when confronted with our habitual knee-jerk emotions of desiring, envying and expecting, is to ask ourselves: Is it important? If we are honest, we will quickly see, in face of life's reality, that it is not important and we will be able to disengage, not entirely, perhaps, but disengage enough to restore some equanimity and acceptance to our lives.

Ego, desires and expectations are all wrapped up together. The ego requires defending and promoting ourselves in relation to others. Desire often stems from a need to protect one's self-image, and expectations are, likewise, often self-serving. Craving a substance is, as has been said, a desire that may have become physiological and is probably no longer ego-driven, and expectations for the well-being of another may be detached from the ego, if genuine. By and large, however, a reduction in ego will result in a reduction in desire and in expectations. But since they are intertwined, we may work on restraining one with an impact on the other two. Best yet, we need to be aware of all three, all existing in our minds and all susceptible to our conscious control.

I have been discussing the inborn traits to which we all seemed susceptible, namely egocentricity, yearning, and expecting. This is not an exhaustive list. Other inborn traits which come to mind are, for example, generosity, camaraderie, and sympathy. The expression of the latter traits brings a sense of fulfillment, while the first three bring discontent, regret and disappointment. To achieve contentment and well-being in this life, an intelligent person will try to control and diminish the former traits, allowing the latter traits to flourish.

* * *

Attachment

In discussing desire, I suggested that attachment to a favorable outcome, even for a good cause, could be detrimental to one's peace of mind. This thought can be extended to all attachments. Attachments may expose one to disappointment, hurt and grief.

Why is this so? Why may attachments be invitations to hurt and grief? Fundamentally, because all existing objects, including humans, and especially humans, are subject to change. The whole world is changing. Change is the order of the universe. Mountains and rocks, trees and plants, organizations and relationships and men and women are all in transition. Transition from what they were to what they are. Transition from what they are to what they will be.

One's attachment is fixed, by definition, to an object or person as it is. When the inevitable change occurs, the object of attachment is gone. Take a material object, such as a car, for example. You have seen this gorgeous red BMW convertible and you imagine yourself in it, owning it and possessing it, and you have the ability to acquire it and do acquire it. The BMW has a good reputation as an automobile, but why a red convertible? Once behind the wheel you cannot see it. But others can see it and that is the point. You imagine yourself in it as seen by others. You imagine them having the same envy as you experienced seeing the car and its driver before you bought it. But what a disappointment awaits you as possessor of a new red convertible BMW.

At first, your friends reacted as expected. They admired your car appropriately. But once done they never comment again. They take you and your car for granted. Meanwhile, you surreptitiously look around in traffic to see whether others are looking at you with envy. You find that, since they are not your friends, they have no obligation to stoke your pride. They look right through you without notice of you, except as another vehicle in traffic. Now you are sitting in traffic in your car, which is gray on the inside, not red, and which in traffic performs no better than any other car. And so the joyride is over. Your personal gratification was short-lived and already you have lost interest. What's more, and this is of significance, in a short time, your car is no longer new. You are no longer the owner of a new red BMW. You are the owner of a used car. The red has faded a bit, there are some nicks in it and the mechanism for lowering the top gets stuck from time to time. This is no great problem, because you find there are very few occasions when driving with the top down is agreeable. The new red BMW convertible has already become something different than it was when you bought it.

One's attachment to an object may be transferred to the changed object, but that which has changed has gone forever. It is beyond restoration. If change is small and gradual, then transference of attachment to the changed object is facilitated. It becomes almost automatic until enough change has occurred to force its reality upon one's awareness. By then, transference may no longer be possible and loss is experienced.

Change will produce a sense of loss, but not necessarily of grief and hurt. It is also possible that change will be seen as change for the better. That which is lost is acknowledged, but the new compensates. It is seen as improvement. Growth is the kind of change we usually welcome, except of course in the case of malignancy.

Nevertheless, the underlying current of change for both material and living forms is ultimately toward dissolution. The form dissolves, the elements dispersed. However, during the period of growth of living organisms, the forces of dissolution are overwhelmed. Then, as growth subsides, dissolution emerges. Perhaps there is a moment of equilibrium; I do not know. It appears to me that the rate of dissolution is slow and small at first and is ignored. It accelerates as it approaches death. It no longer can be ignored.

Although death is inevitable, the process of dissolution can be restrained and made less humiliating by the individual who understands early in life that growth offsets dissolution. Growth is always a possibility for every human being. The intelligent person will seek continued growth in view of the alternative, misery and remorse. Such a person will seek growth in understanding, growth in knowledge, growth in virtue and growth in psychological independence, which is to say contentment and peace of mind.

For us, permanence and impermanence, change and changelessness are perceptions we have. Those perceptions themselves change. For the young person, everything and everybody is permanent and changeless. For an older person like me, everything is in rapid change, except that change itself is changeless. However, the first changes in one's experience of life are shocking: the dissolution of one's family, the loss of a friend, the theft of a bicycle, the death of a teacher. There is bewilderment, frustration, anger and anguish. But for the older person, it is a sad shrug of the shoulders. To the young person, the older person seems heartless. However, for the older person, change has taken its toll. It has forced detachment, not heartlessness.

Since the detached person may be thought of as heartless, we may prefer attachment and caring no matter what might be the future loss and heartache to ourselves. This to my mind is misguided. Attachment is often dependence, becoming a need.

One may cherish another without attachment. Love and detachment are not antithetical. Warm-heartedness, enthusiasm and supportiveness do not demand attachment. Interest and concern do not demand attachment. Congeniality and commonality of taste, attitudes and values do not demand attachment. In fact, attachment can load a relationship with an unbearable weight of expectation and demand. Attachment can lead to jealousy and, of course, hurt.

Detachment in personal relationships is not heartless. Detachment is the path of wisdom, beneficial to one's self and to others. I remember a film I once saw of Mother Teresa visiting patients in one of her charitable clinics. She stopped at each bed, placed her hands beside each face, looked the individual in the eyes and gave them all her love and support. She blessed them and then--she moved on.

In conclusion, I would like to briefly summarize what I have said about attachment and detachment. First of all, I observed that attachments are not conducive to peace of mind. This is so, because material objects and living things are all in transition. Consequently, in time, the object of one's attachment will change. The original object of attachment will be lost. However, one may shift one's attachment successively to the changing object of one's original attachment. Ultimately, loss, and perhaps grief, will ensue.

Transition is toward dissolution. Creation and growth forestall the forces of dissolution until their work is done. One may ameliorate the impact of one's own dissolution by continuing to grow, intellectually, morally, and spiritually.

The antidote to attachment is detachment. Detachment is not heartless. It is the path of wisdom and to contentment and well-being.

Chapter III

Will, Choice, and Action

Underlying my discussion, thus far, is the notion we can change our lives, if we want to. This assumes that we are dissatisfied with our lives as we are now living them. Many of us are dissatisfied, but out of an odd perversity we do not want to change them. The reason for this apparent perversity is, of course, inertia. It also arises from a reluctance to act out of character. How can one suddenly begin being solicitous of all others, standing aside in every line, never being annoyed in traffic, being tolerant of public rudeness and vulgarity, forgiving the thoughtlessness of spouse and children, avoiding all derogatory remarks about others and remaining silent about one's own self? Regarding the last, not talking about oneself, one need not worry. No one will notice when you stop volunteering information about yourself. If others are really interested they will ask; but in my experience we will wait a long time to be asked. On the other hand, we can ask others about themselves and they will melt before your eyes in appreciation. I believe it is far better to ask than to be asked, better for ourselves.

I want to return, though, to the matter of suddenly stepping out of character. It is interesting to note that, although the Buddha saw universal human suffering, he customarily addressed monks, persons already identified with an aberrant lifestyle, dedicated to perfecting themselves. They, of course, wore special clothing, identifying themselves as holy men and women, and the rest of society paid deference to them, providing their living for them. That is hardly our case. We dress conventionally, have spouses and children and jobs, and cars and computers and supermarkets. We, nevertheless, suspect that there is something more to life, because we often live with anxiety, irritation, harassment, boredom and fatigue. Yet we cannot suddenly become nuns or monks or hermits in order to find peace and contentment. Nevertheless, I come along and insist that you can change your life by changing yourself. The odds against doing that seem very high, but I say do it little by little, no vows, no proclamations, no exterior changes, just a personal, private resolve to become a mature person, a person of goodwill. Step-by-step and incrementally change yourself, not your appearance, not your job, not your spouse. Rather, change your inner self. Try an experiment in living as Gandhi described his life. If you try it, you will like it, I believe. It will grow on you, and your experience of your only life will flower.

In trying to make it practical and doable, I may be sugarcoating a difficult reality. Change may not come as easily as I have made it sound. For most of us, it is perhaps a more difficult path than I have implied. I have said that we must first want to change ourselves in order to change our living experience, a want tantamount to need. It is this need that provides the determination and the willpower to change our selves. Let's look at willpower.

Like energy--say, for example, energy from the sun--willpower is not something you can put your finger on, you can measure, something that is allocated in different proportions to different people. Willpower can only be manifested in voluntary action. What do we do? Do our actions show consistency and direction?

When we are identifying specific actions as examples of willpower, they are usually actions which have rejected immediate gratification for more distant and, perhaps, less tangible rewards.

Every action we take represents a choice. We could have chosen a different action. We hear people say, "I don't know what made me do that," suggesting that some power outside us made us do what we did. We had no choice. There are circumstances in which this can be fairly and convincingly argued--under duress, for example--and yet it can also be argued that even under duress we have a choice. We can refuse to comply and take the consequence no matter how horrifying.

The reality is that all of us can be induced or compelled to take action against our will, but how often and how honestly? By asking how honestly, I mean can we honestly say that there was no alternative--in other words, no choice? It is not often that we are forced at gunpoint to take action against our wills. It is more often the case that we took the action we wanted to take, no matter what the rationale. We do have a choice almost all the time.

Having choice is both a burden and an opportunity. The huge majority of our actions are reactions made without deliberate choice and, hence, without burden. We act thoughtlessly, depending largely on habit, training and emulation for guidance, and we live thoughtless lives. But herein lies a problem. That we do not think beforehand about most of our actions does not mean we cannot or ought not. Many of our reactions are not only thoughtless, but harmful to ourselves and others as well. We need to think about them. You might say we cannot have a mental debate weighing the pros and cons of our every action. It is tiresome. It is time-consuming. We prefer to act quickly without too much thought. Thus it is that we lose control of our lives.

Here I will, again, digress. It is said that we use only a fraction of our brains, or call it our mental capacity. If this is true, it seems to me a strange anomaly in the theory of evolution. If species developed as a result of mutation and adaptation to unique environmental conditions over long periods of time, how is it that the human species developed a generalized excess capacity of brain in a relatively short period of time? This is simply a question and is not intended to imply divine creation. My point is that human intelligence, commonly assumed to be seated in the brain, is enormous compared with other animal intelligence and other animal brains. This being so, ought not human existence be enormously different from other animal existence? But is it? I suppose you will say of course it is. We drive automobiles, communicate visually and audibly across the planet, prolong human life medically, and some of us can even control and plan how many babies we have. No animals I know of intentionally practice birth control. There are obviously hundreds of mechanical appliances that make our lives different from other animals' in terms of physical comfort and convenience. But can we say that our subjective experience of life is better than animals' experience of life even with our large brains? We can never know. But what can we surmise?

We may surmise, I believe, that animals live in the present. I often wonder if a bird knows it will get dark, or if it simply accepts darkness when it becomes dark. Even if a bird has some premonition of darkness in a dwindling light, it is unlikely that it anticipates darkness at high noon. Birds do not worry a lot. But it is also the case that birds often die in stormy weather that they failed to anticipate. And so do many humans.

With greater intelligence, we humans can, in the present, anticipate the future. And yet, our observer from outer space would probably not notice in human behavior much difference between birds and humans. We continue to build homes, and towns and cities under active volcanoes, as though no eruptions will come; build new housing developments in water drainages, as though no flood will come; consume trees in new housing, as though barrenness, dust, erosion, and drought will never come. It is high noon for men, and in the personal realm as well. The lender will never come to the borrower, the cancer will never come to the smoker, the truth will never reveal the lies. I believe many humans live their lives with the same intelligence as an animal lives its life, despite men's enormous superiority in intellectual capacity. It is high noon for most humans. The darkness will never come. Death is on the back burner.

It seems to me that a human being with more intelligence than he uses and unlike a bird soaring high in the still-lit sky, such a being can put two and two together, can anticipate the darkness coming, and can foresee the consequences of actions taken. Given that capacity, a human being can act with intelligence, not just instinctively. In other words, a human being can choose to act wisely. Acting wisely, humans may have a life experience sublime. Otherwise, I believe the human life experience is little different than that of other living creatures.

Returning now to the idea that we have choice and can determine our actions, how does that capacity enable us to change our lives? How do we know what choices to make? Basically, we can arrive at certain general guidelines to which we can refer in making choices. These are derived from knowing how we want to live and what actions are required to achieve our intent. For example, if our intent is to achieve more harmonious and less stressed relations with others, we will refrain from gossiping, especially from making disparaging remarks about others. We will avoid confrontations over trivia, and we will be thoughtful of others and courteous towards others.

Incidentally, I believe it is important not to insist on being right in a disagreement with another. Let the other person be right. It cannot hurt you. In fact, refusing to debate, conceding to another's point of view or another's interpretation of an event will leave you calm, unperturbed and on amicable relations with the other. Besides, it is almost impossible to persuade others against themselves. So let it be. But do it with grace, not grudgingly, disparagingly, not with an "okay this time" attitude. Do it sincerely, because there is always some truth on the other side and with an open mind you may have learned something from the other person's position. No one is all right, even you.

Perhaps, an open mind, above all else, eases tensions and rewards us. With an open mind, we find tolerance, acceptance and perspective. Rigidity of mind brings us anguish, because the world ignores and violates our fixed beliefs, again and again. We may resort to denial and then find ourselves at odds with all around us, angry and isolated. This may be overdrawn, but I'm sure that an open and flexible mind is a happier mind than a rigid and closed mind. An open mind allows us, more readily, to make choices in compliance with our guidelines.

* * *

Honesty

The first sign of corrupt morals is the banishing of the truth, ...being truthful is the beginning of any great virtue.
--Michel de Montaigne

As humans, we can talk and we have a language, in contrast to other animals. What a fantastic difference it makes in our lives and relations with other humans. The benefits I need not enumerate. But enormous liabilities and difficulties also accompany the gift of speech. We can say anything, admiring words, encouraging words, loving words, poetic words, profane words, hurtful words or dishonest words. Since the words uttered are entirely of our own choice, none are more tempting than false words. False words are available to mislead and deceive others. They are incredibly tempting because they are an easy way to protect or advantage ourselves. Just think of it! Any time, all the time, the words are there for us to say them, words that will divert, mislead, or misinform others to our benefit. What a temptation, no effort, they can slip out so easily. And who among us can resist?

But how important it is to resist! The whole fabric of society and human relations, one with another, depends on our reliance upon one another. So fragile is this reliance that we have developed an elaborate system of contracts, background checks and penalties to bolster reliance on one another's word, especially in commerce. In less institutionalized relations, we learn, as we grow older, to take almost everything we hear with a grain of salt. When we reach old age, we take it with a spoon of salt. It is just too great a temptation for the human tongue to resist, always, this easy dodge, easy exploitation of one's advantage. Incidentally, one of the most common forms of dishonesty is exaggeration. Misfortune to horror, misunderstanding becomes a crime, awkwardness a big laugh. Not really an untruth, just a dollop here and there of omitted or added information. The narrator has gained something, one can be sure.

The problem with lying, as has often been pointed out, is remembering the lie. A lie is not a onetime thing, but lives on and spreads its tendrils. And the liar must remember, because a lie requires other lies to cover it. The liar becomes apprehensive, because as long as the lie and its offspring are out there, there is the possibility of a slip of the tongue in a relaxed and forgetful moment. Lying produces anxiety, requires constant vigilance, carries a load of guilt and destroys relationships. Why would any intelligent person lie?

But these aspects of lying are not the reason I brought up the subject at this point. Aside from the characteristics of a lie in the exterior world, there is the more important dishonesty of lying to oneself. Not one single step toward contentment and well-being will be achieved if one lies to oneself. And how hard it is not to lie to oneself. Lying to oneself is even more tempting than lying to others. There is no accountability when lying to oneself, and no fear of discovery. So we lie to ourselves all the time. We tell ourselves that we did not mean to offend, we are not to be blamed for being late, we tried our very best, we worked as hard as we could, there was nothing else we could have done, we were only trying to help, we are too tired to do a chore, the timing is not right, tomorrow will be time enough, we only have ice cream occasionally and anyhow we deserve it tonight. Every one of these lies we know is a lie and yet we will not confront the truth. Not confronting the truth, not being honest with ourselves, we lose our self-respect. Lying to ourselves becomes habitual, yet we lament our lack of accomplishment. I knew of a teacher once, who said to students who presented poor papers late, "That's your excuse; now tell me your reason."

Tell me your reason, the real reason. That is a tough one, because if one told the real reason, it might be laziness, slovenliness, lack of self-discipline, lack of intent, lack of awareness, lack of commitment or lack of intelligence. We do not readily confront the real reasons, but if we do not, we will not make the most of our one life. We will regret that we fooled away so much of it, fooling ourselves.

* * *

Self-Discipline

Self-discipline is akin to lying. It requires self-discipline not to lie, especially not to lie to ourselves. Unlike lying, which is tempting because it is so easy, self-discipline can be repugnant because it is so difficult. I once found it a repugnant notion, because it conjured for me images of rigidity, inflexibility, hypocrisy, and self-righteousness. Self-discipline, in my mind, was used to demonstrate superiority to other weaker souls. But now, I look upon self-discipline in an entirely different light, because I think of it differently. I think of self-discipline as an entirely private matter. It should, I believe, be approached humbly and without notice. No vows, no public announcements. It is something that one decides is worth developing, but knows fully well there will be omissions and relapses. These omissions and relapses are not subjects for public confession or judgment. They are subjects for one's own observation. They do not sabotage one's resolve. One is not infallible, nor a failure. One does not conclude that self-discipline is not for one. One does not give up. This would be self-deceit. If other human beings can practice self-discipline, then it is within our own human capacity to do so as well.

What is self-discipline? My dictionary defines self-discipline as "discipline and training of oneself, usually for improvement." And so, apparently, the dictionary meaning of self-discipline is essentially self-training. But this is not entirely what I have in mind by the notion of self-discipline. Perhaps I should be using a different expression, but for me, self-discipline is a practice more than training. It is a practice involving restraint in action and from action.

Self-discipline involves habituation. Having self-discipline, we do some actions or refrain from doing other actions, habitually. We habitually acknowledge our own mistakes and habitually refrain from pointing out to others their mistakes. Other examples more pertinent might be that we habitually refrain from thoughts about what others think of us; therefore, we refrain from actions which respond to our speculations about what others will approve or disapprove. We habitually avoid use of the first person singular as an expression of our ego and self-importance, and we habitually avoid having expectations for the good or bad behavior of others as we see it. Some examples of self-discipline in action include acting with respect and courtesy toward others, exercising our bodies with vigor and focus to preserve our health, and also eating wholesome food to preserve our health. It is because of these actions that I want to stick with the expression "self-discipline." Otherwise, I might have used the phrase "self-restraint." So much of self-discipline, as I see it, has to do with restraint of our emotions, restraint of our language, restraint of our involvement in the world of otherness and even restraint of our wandering minds.

Earlier, I wrote that self-discipline is difficult. It is until one discovers a secret. That secret is that self-discipline gets easier and easier as one practices it. I think it gets easier because of its rewards. We feel so much better. We develop a sense of self-control, of self-respect, of security and contentment. With self-discipline, one owns one's life. Without it, one becomes the object, not the subject of one's life, a victim of one's own appetites, fantasies, misconceptions and dishonesty. Self-discipline pays high dividends, which invite persistence and finally habitualness. When it becomes habit, it no longer demands resolve. It is no longer difficult. I wish very much that everyone could understand this. It is the difference between humans and other animals. It is the difference between childhood and maturity. It is the difference between suffering and well-being.

With self-discipline, we hold our tongue; with self-discipline, we wait; with self-discipline, we do without; with self-discipline, we gain consistency; with self-discipline, we withdraw from speculation; with self-discipline, we become focused. "How dull," you say. And I say, try it and see. Life becomes lighter, and, I believe, we are happier, because so many of our anxieties, yearnings, illness, accidents, disappointments and hurts have vanished or at least have been marginalized. Knowing what we have to do to make our lives enjoyable and having the conviction and self-discipline to do what is required pays off, not later in heaven, but now on Earth. We do what we have to do, not because it is commanded by divine mandate and preached by the ordained, but rather because our intelligence and reason, given the reality of our existence, guide us. We cherish our one life, and with intelligence, cultivate it.

* * *

Forgetting

In the foregoing, numerous guidelines emerged from our discussion of self-discipline. Self-discipline is exercised at the moment of choice, when we choose to act, not to act or how to act. I have said we can be guided in our choices by reference to our guidelines. The problem is forgetting our guidelines and our commitment to them.

Forgetting is the enemy. I use the word "enemy" with some reluctance. I am not sure that we harbor enemies within us. In fact, forgetfulness is also our friend, a great servant, helping us to live. In forgetfulness, we continue to act out our daily lives, momentarily oblivious to past loss, hurt, or death. As time passes, memories sink deeper into our so-called unconsciousness, our forgetfulness. But the same forgetfulness can sabotage us in our efforts to change ourselves. We overcome forgetfulness by remembering.

It is difficult in the beginning, remembering to remember. Impulse and habit are hard to override, partly because they are so fast. You have already done what you did not want to do by the time you remember. But with perseverance, you will remember your guidelines more often and remember them before you act more often. I say this because it is what I have experienced. I believe I have had some success in bringing my actions into conformity with my adopted guidelines, though I still react too often in ways I regret. As I have said, I believe we need to practice living our guidelines. It is not a matter of conversion or rebirth or instant salvation. It is rather a matter of practice and focus. Remembering one's guidelines. Not forgetting.

One guideline that is of particular significance to our living experience is the practice of courtesy toward others.

* * *

Courtesy

Courtesy is expressed in good manners, yet good manners are an outmoded and almost forgotten topic today. I think that people have come to see good manners as an affectation of the elite or the hypocrisy of the rich. In any event, it seems to me that the notion of good manners is almost lost from consciousness in our society. Yet good manners are basically a demonstration of respect and care for others. The opposite, rudeness, is disrespect, a lack of caring for others and worse, a ruthless imposition of self-interest above all others. Rudeness in human behavior is akin to animal behavior, pigs at the trough.

Among some human beings throughout the ages, there has always been the belief that one's greatest satisfaction in life is caring for others. As far as I know, human beings have always lived in families, bands, tribes, or larger conglomerations. It is, perhaps, an evolutionary adaptation that humans have developed a capacity for caring for one another. No society of humans can survive without the glue of civility and caring. There is ample and terrible evidence of this in societies torn by strife, massacre and tyranny throughout history and today. It is a stretch to attribute the dissolution of societies to a lack of civility alone. On the other hand, one might argue that if everyone cared for others everywhere, there would be much less social strife. The point of this risky digression into social speculation is to emphasize the reasonable self-interest and necessity of our caring and thoughtfulness towards others: being courteous. It not only makes our daily living so much more enjoyable, it also promotes our personal security and good feeling. If we follow our guidelines, we will be courteous in our actions towards others for reasons we understand.

The words I have been using--"caring," "courtesy," "thoughtfulness," even "good manners"-- are all encompassed in a single word, the word "love." But the word "love" is so laden with sentimentality and passion that I hesitate to use it. However, I will return to love later. Love has the capacity to change our lives.

Chapter IV

Marriage

Meanwhile, my thoughts turn to a subject involving caring, courtesy, thoughtfulness and love. I am thinking of marriage and other relationships involving sex. I am equally reluctant to express my thoughts on this subject, because it is so central and so loaded with expert opinion. There are trained marriage counselors galore, and every magazine at the checkout has the latest explicit information on sex and how to lose weight. I suppose the two are related. In any event, I venture into this minefield with trepidation.

I begin with sexual relationships outside of marriage. They were unheard of when and where I grew up, at least by me, as a young person. I cannot be sure what knowing adults knew, but at a later time in my life, I read bold suggestions that trial marriage might be a way to reduce the rapidly rising divorce rate. It seemed to be a logical proposal to me, but not one that had any chance of acceptance. In fact, it never found acceptance in the sense that couples would enter it, publicly, as a trial marriage.

However, as we all know, couples now commonly live together, outside of marriage. Not secretly as they once did, but openly. They talk freely of their relationship, and of their partners. They entertain friends and families as a couple and are entertained as a couple in return. Together they visit the parental guestroom for extended visits and not even the grandparents raise an eyebrow. The only problem is naming the relationship and, especially, what to call the other. "Fiancée" or "fiancé," depending on gender, was popular for a while, giving a nod to an earlier code of morality. Now more often a member of the couple simply refers to the other by name, leaving new acquaintances to speculate as to their relationship, usually not hard to do.

These relationships do not interest me particularly, except as a social phenomenon. It is interesting how easily the bedrock, the even sacred tenets of Western morality collapsed in a period of perhaps twenty-five years. The grandparents folded their tents and slipped away in the night only to return with humble smiles of acceptance. And nothing earthshaking has happened as a consequence.

These relationships have no function other than sexual companionship. They are unceremoniously consummated, often as a convenient living arrangement with only the inconvenience of moving in the furniture. They break up easily with the similar inconvenience of moving out the furniture. Unfortunately, when they break up, more than likely one of the couple is hurt, probably the woman. If young people could know how short life is, how important it is to live it wisely, they might want to use care and discretion and a large pinch of reluctance before entering a live-in sexual relationship. Since for many the attractiveness of such a relationship is in what one is leaving, as much as what one is entering, the capacity for clear-sightedness is obscured. It is important, I believe, to be sure of a mutuality of interest, goals, temperament, tastes and background before becoming enmeshed out of convenience. These are the same ingredients that marriage includes. In that sense, a good relationship may, after the fact, have been a trial marriage.

There is one great difference between a relationship "out of wedlock," as it was once aptly called, and a marriage. This difference is in purpose. Marriage is for the purpose of raising children. An informal sexual relationship might be to explore marriage, but is more often for convenience. It is not for having children. It does not provide the stability essential to child welfare, the commitment of both parents, the forethought and planning that a marriage should provide. Wanton wandering in and out of relationships based on the ephemeral ground of sexual desire and convenience is an extravagant waste of one's life, emotionally, mentally, and physically.

If, on the other hand, a relationship is founded on mutuality, and has endured over time, why marry? At one time, I would have said no need whatever. I have come to modify the position largely because of children. I have observed that children seem to have an instinctive vested interest in the bonding of their parents. It arises, I believe, out of the human child's prolonged helplessness before achieving maturity. The child's desperate need requires security. Two parents are better than one and surrogates seldom suffice.

Marriage tends to strengthen the bond between two partners. Marriage is official bonding, public bonding, and legal bonding. It creates a "Mrs." and "Mr." between opposite sexes. It gives children a family name and yes, it may be dissolved, but with a whole lot more difficulty than simply moving out the furniture.

Divorce rates have risen over the years, but I believe that the prognosis for a particular marriage might improve if marriage is better understood and the commitment required seriously considered. The problem, I believe, is the basis for marriage. Romantic passionate love is considered compelling and sufficient. It is the worst possible basis for a marriage, in my thinking. It has been said that romantic love has a lifetime of about two years. My observation collaborates this estimate. What a flimsy, whimsical, emotional, and irrational ground for marriage! No wonder there is so much heartache, anger, distress, and disappointment when the marriage dissolves. An infantile bubble has burst and nobody knows why. Only the photo album lasts--lace and virginal white, bouquets and gifts, feasting and dancing, kisses and hugs and tears, all memorialized by Kodak, passionate, romantic love achieving its climax in the wedding. Afterwards, the couple is left deflated, face-to-face in the vacuity of fulfilled romantic love. On the other hand, consider the following on friendship:

> *Our tastes and aims and views were identical—and that is where the essence of friendship lies.*

> *Friendship may be defined as a complete identity of feeling about all things in heaven and earth, an identity, which is strengthened by mutual good will and affection.*

> *Friendship, then, both adds a brighter glow to prosperity and relieves adversity by dividing and sharing the burden. And another of its very remarkable advantages is this, it is unique because of the bright rays of hope it projects into the future: it never allows the spirit to falter or fall.*

> *But when there is real friendship, no element of falsity of pretense can possibly enter into the matter. Friendship cannot help being genuine*

and sincere all through. It comes from
a feeling of affection, an inclination of
the heart.

For goodwill is established by love
quite independently of any calculation
of profit: it is from love, <u>amor</u>, that the
word of friendship <u>amicitia</u> is derived.

Reading these words several years ago, I kept thinking, should not this description of friendship also be a description of marriage? I have excerpted the thoughts on friendship which you have just read from *On the Good Life* by Cicero and from his chapter, "On Friendship." Cicero was a Roman orator and statesman born in 106 B.C. He died in 43 B.C. The thing that fascinates me about reading the Romans of Cicero's era is how contemporary their lives were with ours today. Perhaps this reflects the fact that they were living at a time of Roman power and prosperity as we are in America today. The circumstances surrounding a life lived in either epoch are similar. The thoughts of enlightened Romans are, therefore, of interest to us. Incidentally, Cicero thought of friendship as a relationship between men, usually influential men of like prominence and interests. Apparently, Cicero did not think of his wife as a friend. She was a wife, something very different. In this, the world has not changed much in the intervening 2000 years. However, recently an acquaintance of mine, a woman in her 30s, told me of her upcoming marriage and here is how she said it: "I'm marrying my best friend." Although I did not say it, I wanted to say, "Right on! I bet your marriage will be a success." Instead, I mumbled the conventional good wishes, not being certain that I understood what she meant by "friend."

What did Cicero mean? He wrote, "Friendship may be defined as a complete identity of feeling about all things in heaven and earth: an identity which is strengthened by mutual goodwill and affection." You have read it above. First of all, there needs to be commonality of taste, interests, values, and aspirations. More than that, Cicero wrote of "an identity of feeling" by which he might have meant feeling toward each other, toward others, toward family, and toward life and death.

A commonality of interests would be, I believe, largely a function of a similarity in childhood and youthful family and school experiences. And an identity of feeling implies, I suppose, similar temperaments and dispositions or, at least, compatible reactions to life's demands. Unsaid but important is admiration. Friends must admire each other's intelligence, capability, accomplishments and character. Friends inspire each other by example. A marriage should be based on friendship, a friendship such as Cicero described it.

I have been emphasizing friendship as a basis for marriage, but marriage itself implies more. Marriage is more than simply friendship. Marriage requires a long-term commitment to mutual support: a duty to provide economic and physical support for one's spouse and children. In earlier times this commitment implied gender roles: on the part of the wife, all of the health and care duties of clothing, cooking and cleaning; on the part of the husband, all of the out of the home income producing activities. Today, these roles have become blurred. Each partner works for income outside the home, and the in-house duties are shared, part time, by both partners, or they still fall largely on the wife in addition to her outside job, or they are radically neglected. In the event of the incapacity of one of the partners, the full load falls on the shoulders of the other. This is the marriage obligation. Marriage does not provide equity. It binds the partners to their vows declared on a balmy June afternoon years before. It does so for the security of the children. But these marriage vows and duties may not always be experienced only as burdens. They may also be self-fulfilling and rewarding. They may be borne gladly on the shoulders of love. Thus, new generations come to be.

Chapter V

The Meaning of Love

What do I mean by love? I suspect that what flashes first in one's mind is romantic love, Valentine's love. Beyond romantic love one thinks of the dutiful love of parents and children.

In the first instance of romantic love, I believe it is biological, a compulsive desire to breed. It assures the continuance of the species. It is equally compelling among all animals, although not as obsessive and prolonged among other animals as among humans. Among animals, romantic love is only inflamed when the female is in estrus, which lasts only a number of days. Meanwhile, the business of life dominates the animal's attention, which is of course helpful, to say the least, to its survival. An animal cannot afford days and months of mooning over a beloved one. Romance is short-lived and spasmodic for most animals. The purpose is fulfilled quickly and quickly forgotten. The purpose? Sexual intercourse.

Does this imply that the purpose of romantic love among humans is also sexual intercourse? Of course it does. This is the bottom line. In many cultures or in different strata within cultures, the bottom line is a fact and is taken as a matter of fact.

Does not romantic love elevate human love above animal love? Perhaps it does, but only in its duration. How do we know, for instance, that Jack the skunk is not romantically and passionately in love with his intended mate, the one and only Julia, at least for the inspiring moments before consummation?

The problem, the very big problem, for humans is that romantic love, while usually more enduring than Jack the skunk's romantic love, is also of relatively short duration. As I have previously pointed out, romantic love has been observed to last approximately two years. It ends either in distress and separation, or ennui and duty, or it undergoes metamorphosis and becomes mature love. In mature love, humans find a greater distinction than in romantic love compared with other animals.

Parental love, especially a mother's love for her children, is very different than romantic love. Parental love has a different purpose. It provides nurturing and care for children. It does not seek gratification, although it provides gratification. It seeks the welfare of the child. It is closer to mature love. At the same time, the love of adult children for their parents and grandparents may also be closer to mature love than romantic love, if genuine. All too often it is mixed up with custom, duty and future benefit. If genuine, or to the extent that it is not self-serving, it is an elevated form of human love. I have never known a dog that loved his grandfather.

And so romantic love is hardly distinguished from all animal sexual attraction, except that it is dressed up in lace and is sometimes delayed in fulfillment. Before the sexual revolution, women, especially those of means and delicate dispositions, cultivated and prolonged romantic love until there was appropriate evidence and assurance of support in the years ahead for themselves and for their children. However, women were freed from innocence and virtue by the sexual revolution, often to become single mothers.

Now, the elusive nature of mature love seeks description. Mature love is altogether different than romantic, passionate, sexual love. To make this distinction, I will begin by telling what I think mature human love is not. Mature love is not infatuation with a potential sex partner. It does not demand exclusive possession, nor reward. It is not generated out of personal need or desire. It is not object-specific and, therefore, is not limited, for example, to a single person. Mature love does not languish, because it is not attachment to a single object, which inevitably changes with time and no longer satisfies the need and the desire out of which it arose. Therefore, mature human love is not transmigratory. It does not pulsate.

A description of what mature love is emerges from the description of that which it is not. Mature love is, I believe, an inclusive, general love rather than specific, exclusive love. Mature love seeks no reward, no return or obligation. It serves no personal need and gives rise to no attachments. It is an inner state of being that is open, nonjudgmental, perceptive and empathetic. It stands in the shoes of the other. It wishes well.

This description of mature love is a concept in my mind and now, perhaps, in yours. It is, perhaps, an example of the Platonic Idea, having existence regardless of you and me. In any event, it is unattainable.

I do not believe that many of us can become living embodiments of true, mature love. But we can try. We can try by taking little steps and by remembering who it is we want to be, remembering that we have one life to live. To live it peacefully and fully in contentment and well-being, we need to quench desire and ego and now, additionally, to nurture our capacity for mature love.

But notice that love is an anecdote to ego and desire. It is impossible to believe that one who is well-wishing toward others, desires anything that is disadvantageous to others, or exploits others, or humiliates others, or promotes invidious comparison. Such desires, usually for material goods or positions of superior power, are ego-driven. Thus mature love diminishes both, both ego and desire. Mature love facilitates or even supplants our efforts to remember and the self-discipline we practice to diminish our thoughtless impulses towards self-promotion as we imagine it. We do not have to reason it. We simply feel it. Mature love comes naturally from the heart-- our work is diminished.

I have also said that we need to nurture mature love, and I believe we do. Nurturing love is, however, quite different than restraining selfishness. So the situation is, perhaps, analogous to a pair of gloves.

The right and left hands are different, but they are most effective used together. We need to remember to restrain our impulses towards aggrandizement and nurture our impulses towards generosity.

* * *

The Difficulties in Loving

I have said that mature love is general love, all-inclusive love. But can you love everyone? Can you love the rude, vulgar or profane? Can you love the pusher, the grabber, and the inconsiderate? Can you love the braggart, the dishonest among whom many are braggarts? Can you love the swindler, especially if you are the victim, or the murderer, again, especially if you are the victim?

I believe, as I have previously said, that the validity or usefulness of a concept is strained in the extreme case. It is often claimed by the proposer of the extreme case that, because of the difficulty it creates, the usefulness of the concept as a whole is destroyed. I believe this is not true. When one thinks of the bell curve, as an example, one realizes that the large majority of cases of whatever description are clustered at the midpoint between the opposite extremes. It is here in the middle that the experience of life for most of us is also clustered. So whether we can love our attacker or not, whether we want to or not, is an extreme case. That one cannot love one's attacker in a murderous situation does not invalidate the concept of mature love as a guiding principle of the good life.

I think, then, that a more realistic test of the possibility of a general inclusive love is in our frequent encounter with disregard, disregard for ourselves by others and disregard for the social fabric. In the first case, it is our ego that has been trampled, and we can deal with that by realizing it. We can suppress our feeling of resentment and excuse the other on whatever grounds, ignorance, thoughtlessness or self-absorption. We will feel better at once for having done so.

It seems to me, however, that disregard by others for the social fabric, as we see it, is a more difficult problem. The very ground for preserving civility in society is the use of disapproval for infractions of accepted behavioral norms. It is obvious that these norms, these rules of the game, vary from one society to another and from the sorority house to the nation's capital. It is also obvious that no society can function without codes of behavior. Thus, a violation of these codes represents a threat to the existing society and poses a dilemma for a general all-encompassing mature love.

Is it our duty to support the rules of society for the purpose of survival? And can we be selective about which rules to support, those that protect one's personal interest, or those one perceives as protecting the general interest? Certainly, we would agree that, if there is a duty, it is to protect the general interest. That would be the only choice for mature love. What about the method of support and protection? The most effective method is rejection. We shut out the transgressor. We withdraw our acceptance, our welcome, and our goodwill. We make clear our disapproval. But is this compatible with nonjudgmental and unconditional mature love?

I think there is a way around our dilemma. We feel a duty to preserve civility and in order to do that, we feel obliged to censor, admonish, and reject violators. We are often incensed and angry and outraged, and we burn within. What a pity. We hurt only ourselves. Avoiding these destructive feelings, we need not abdicate our duty. We may rebuke and reprimand if called for, but with an attitude of goodwill, with faith in redemption and with understanding. When we do this, suddenly the stress is gone and the incident becomes a loving one, no longer a threatening one. It is soon forgotten, while duty was still met.

> *People never tire of any one who is not*
> *bent upon comparison.*
> *-- Lao Tzu*

But unconditional mature love may be tested in more subtle ways. We constantly discriminate between more or less agreeable objects and circumstances. A discriminating taste, or eye, or mind is generally applauded and seen as a result of training, education or experience. The expert is a connoisseur of art or wine who makes distinctions among objects based on technique and detail. He judges, chooses and rejects. And this is true among living things as well. Dogs and cats and horses, likewise, are appraised. The dog fancier discriminates between breeds and, within a breed, between individual dogs. There is an idea, a standard, for the perfect dog of that breed. Each individual dog, while falling short of the perfect dog, is judged for its approximation. The closer to the standard, the more acceptable is an individual dog to the discriminating judge, and the greater his favor. Other dogs are neglected or at least ignored. But it seems to me that every dog shares equally the essence of being a dog, both the purebred and the crossbreed. Nevertheless, we do not fault the judge for selecting among dogs his favorite and rejecting the others. There was a time in my life when I occasionally attended dog shows. I was pleased for the winner, but my heart went out to the rejected, the underdogs.

There is a point to all this. Suppose through training, education and art, you are a connoisseur of art objects or show animals, and you unavoidably turn your observational and evaluative skills toward human beings. You select favorites among humans according to your standards, and reject others. As a matter of fact, do we not, all of us, consider ourselves expert judges of human nature, and do we not, all of us, choose some human beings for our favor and reject others? Of course we do, but in so doing can we maintain mature love?

Discrimination among humans, rather than among objects and other animals, is called snobbism, racism or sexism. What is the difference? The difference is that discrimination among objects and animals does not hurt the rejected. Among dogs, the proceedings are incomprehensible and, thus, there is no awareness of having been rejected. But among humans, there is awareness of rejection and there is great hurt. Most humans seek recognition. Nothing is so damaging to the human psyche as being ignored. Not counting for anything. In our society, being a loser. There is among humans discrimination and it is hurtful, but can we avoid it? On the basis of color or sex we can make an effort to avoid it, and some progress has been made against discrimination. Legislation prohibiting discrimination exerts a constraint. But in our choice of friends or colleagues, can we avoid discrimination?

In strict logic, I suggest that mature love cannot discriminate, cannot sit in judgment on other human beings. The reality, though, is that most of us will find greater affinity for some people than for others. The task for us, then, is to avoid attributing superiority to those with whom we have affinity and inferiority to others with whom we find less affinity. Certainly we cannot reject, ignore or disparage those outside our group of family and friends. Toward all, mature love remains open and good-willing. But this does not end the difficulties for us who aspire to mature love.

I would guess that most of you reading this have jobs and that your jobs are in organizations: corporations, in most instances. All organizations are hierarchical in structure, and this presents a tremendous obstacle to mature love and goodwill. How can you love your boss? Since in a hierarchical organization you may also be a boss, how do you love your goof-off subordinate? It is hard.

For those caught in the mainstream of our society, the relentless pressures for economic survival erode our best intentions. Our responses are immediate and are conditioned responses to situations created by an economic environment designed for monetary profit, not for love. We are not cloistered. We live in the world.

My suggestions at this point are by now predictable. The best we can do in the hierarchical situation, at the workplace, is to try to put ourselves in the other's shoes. This feat has two aspects. The first, the simpler, is to imagine oneself in the other's role and ask how we might act. This is often helpful and sufficient. It also explains the other's behavior, if we are honest about it. Before we say to ourselves, "I would never do anything like that," we'd better ask ourselves, "Honestly?" Often we will find that in all honesty we might have done the same thing. This will help us to be more tolerant.

The more difficult feat is to try to be the other. To be the other's age and gender and to have the other's family background and schooling and to be in the other's present circumstances. Since we really cannot be the other in all these circumstances, partly because we do not know them, we must resort to what we can know, which is our common humanity. This appeal is often made, and you might react, "I acknowledge our common humanness, but it does not follow that I, therefore, love my boss. As a matter of fact, because I know she is human like me, I demand that she act humanly towards me." This is missing the point. It is not her actions that induce your regard--obviously not. It is her human being-ness, which is the same as yours, her physical necessities, which are met in embarrassing privacy like yours, her need for security, recognition, affirmation, attention and affection just as you need them, and her fear of the loss of her job, health, possessions and life, which match your anxieties. Above all, death is your shared fate. We all live alike with mortality. We are fellow travelers, equally bewildered, wanting desperately to hold hands on our journey, but ashamed to admit it. With this understanding, mature love requires lending a hand to all others, the boss and the subordinate included. It is hard, as I said, but can be done. I know it can.

I now want to turn your attention to a problem you may have, or perhaps, a misunderstanding you may have about my definition of mature love. I have said that mature love is general and inclusive. I have said that it does not demand response in kind or in any other way; it is not for personal benefit in the form of gratitude, indebtedness, or praise. In its truest form it is anonymous. All of this is difficult enough, but you might also interpret unconditional love as self-sacrificing, as manifesting itself in unconditional giving, and I think this is true. I resist the notion, however, that unconditional giving, which is giving without any strings attached, entails, as well, limitless giving. I do not believe that mature love requires opening the door and inviting your neighbors in to strip you of your possessions. We think of the Saints of all time as penniless and, perhaps, we fear that mature love requires impoverishment. I do not think so. Nor do I think we are talking about sainthood.

As strange as it may seem, I would like to unlink loving and giving. Giving gifts is perhaps often linked to loving, because it is simple and simple-minded. If you give a gift, how lovely you are. But also, how easy it is. You buy it and give it. You spend only what you can spare. And custom requires a future gift to you in return. You may protest vigorously that you expect nothing in return, but gifts inevitably create obligations in the minds of the receivers. Consequently, the beneficiary of your largesse, without the means of return in kind, is humiliated. Therefore, gifts given with mature love are token gifts, demonstrating mindfulness and remembrance, but of little intrinsic value. In fact, no material gifts at all are required by mature love. Mature love offers other gifts: the gift of listening, the gift of encouragement, the gift of recognition, the gift of respect, the gift of consolation, the gift of availability, essentially the gifts of caring. These gifts ought not to foster reciprocal dependency. Dependency is a manifestation of need. And love that fosters need is also in response to need. Needy love is not mature love.

I believe, then, that we need not fear loving acts because of burdensome consequences. Mature love is strong and benevolent. It is never a victim of itself or the other. We can begin at once with loving acts without fear. Ultimately, love banishes fear. But fear is groundless to begin with. We gain immeasurably and lose nothing from mature love, though gain and loss are not considerations in mature love. Our understanding and intelligence tell us that goodwill fosters goodwill, eases stress, enriches our relationships with others and automatically diminishes ego and desire. Although we cannot achieve the ideal of mature love, in full, in every instance, some of the practical difficulties and contradictions can be overcome with reasonableness and a good heart.

Very well, you might say, but what about sex? You may accuse me of proposing an unrealistic platonic relationship, which if nothing else, might be the end of the human species. My response is quite simple. Sex is certainly an important facet of a mature love relationship. On the other hand, sex cannot be the vortex of the relationship into which all other facets are sucked, leaving emptiness at the center. Sex between mature lovers is not the personal need of each separately, nor is it the role of one to fulfill the need of the other. Worse still is the objectification of one individual who is seen as bound by the relationship to gratify the other, having, in fact, a duty to do so. Nothing seems to me more abhorrent to the concept of mature love, nothing more contradictory.

When I was young, the fad among sex manuals, which I read surreptitiously and avidly, was to explain to males how they could heighten the sexual enjoyment of females. I thought then and still do today, that it was a revolutionary idea. Males had, I believe, always looked upon females as a source of male pleasure. Even arousing females sexually, when and if ever, was ultimately to enhance male pleasure. Now, I read, although I have not done a survey, that the fad among sex manuals has changed. It is today more enlightened. Each partner now makes known their personal needs and the other responds, in an exchange of favors. Tit for tat, so to speak. To me, this seems incompatible with mature love. A true lover does not have any reward or return in mind. The true lover seeks only the best for the other. The mature lover wants only the comfort, readiness and fulfillment of the other. Lovemaking between mature lovers is selfless. Only then is it truly an act of love.

If you are still with me, I am indebted. My meandering thoughts have taken an especially long path through challenges to mature love. My intent has been to anticipate some of the contradictions within the ideal. I hope in so doing the main thread of my thinking has not been lost. My underlying concern is how to live life and, obviously, I think love enormously enriches one's living experience. With it, I believe, self-restraint and continuing awareness of life's implications are required. However, there is a lighter side of life as well. Not all is earnestness and self-restraint. There is also pleasure and spontaneous joy, the more, the better.

Chapter VI

Pleasure

Pleasure, as it is usually conceived, is not pleasure, but pain. The satisfaction of the craving for food, sweets, alcohol, drugs and tobacco is momentary. Beyond the momentary high, there is a low, and an incremental erosion of the body and mind. Unnoticed at the time, the impairment of the body and the imprisonment of the mind are notched up a little with each new sensational high. We know this, in part, but since gratification is present and payment delayed, we live it up while we can, especially since everyone else is living it up and they are not worried, or so it seems.

We reinforce one another in bad habits, urging upon others intoxicants and debilitating amusements. We invite future pain. We do this not out of maliciousness, but out of ignorance.

There is great confusion and ignorance about pleasure. It is not a product bought and sold and artificially created, including magnified noise. It is not bought in a glass, or on a party ship to the Virgin Islands, or in a beer bottle and a television set on Monday night. Noise, heavy rhythm, pulsating neon, alcohol and suggestive sex will not generate contentment and well-being. To the contrary, they bring only momentary distraction, fleeting fun.

Seeking fun has become a major preoccupation of our times. I do not remember in my past so much emphasis on having fun, nor such a hyped-up effort to prove it to everyone nearby for their admiration and envy. Howls of laughter are not expressions of amusement or pleasure. Pleasure, as I think of it, is not just jokes and consumption. Pleasure is not episodic. It is not derived from isolated, often costly, onetime experiences haunted by an impending return to displeasure. Real pleasure is uplifting, stimulating, recurrent and self-fulfilling. It provides satisfaction and gratification.

Since pleasure is, I think, a legitimate goal of life, it is essential to understand how pleasure is derived. There are two kinds of pleasure in my mind, passive and participatory. We can derive pleasure from simply listening or looking. We can listen to music and look at art or natural scenery and derive great pleasure, but note that this pleasure is occasional and does not involve our participation. This is passive pleasure.

Passive pleasure requires only one's attention. Nevertheless passive pleasure provides greater pleasure when we have done considerable homework previous to listening or looking. When we have done homework, we recognize, understand, and can interpret what we are hearing or seeing. This is true in varying degrees. Some music and art is simplistic. Little understanding is required. Other musical performances or works of art require a high level of understanding. In the first instance, the simplistic, the music or art is more popular. It requires little homework, little cultivation. In the second instance, fewer people derive great pleasure from music and art that can be called classical, but that pleasure will be more enduring and sustaining. This is not to suggest that no pleasure is derived from popular music and art. I am suggesting only that as a pleasure seeker, one should consider the fact that the more effort one exerts to understand and familiarize oneself with music and art, the more pleasure one will derive. Music and art that are complex and refined require more understanding.

Pleasure is also derived from performance entertainment. I have in mind theatre, films and television. But please note that the word "entertainment" is defined in my dictionary as diversion. Entertainment diverts one from one's life and from reality. In the end it drops one back, abruptly, into one's life and reality. For those whose life is empty, boring, or stressful, entertainment is a pain reliever and becomes addictive. It is so easy to switch on the tube and escape one's life by living someone else's life, that of the play actor or sports contestant or newsmaker.

Also, the novel, if a good one, absorbs your mind totally as you live its fictional story. Your own story is probably as absorbing, if it too could be condensed into 300 pages and become as timeless as is a novel. The dramatic events of real life are interspersed with long minutes, days, months and years of routine, and repetitive living chores. But in the novel, as in film and the theatre, there are the flashback and flash-forward that eliminate time and provide you with an absorbing diversion. While enthralled, you are not living your own life, the only one you will ever have. Some entertainment is certainly pleasurable, and I think desirable. But one needs to remember the cost, a loss, however brief or occasional, of one's life. This is the choice we all make, hopefully, not to regret at the last.

There is another important source of pleasure derived from a mix of active participation and passive listening. I have in mind the company of others, companionship, camaraderie, and conviviality. We talk and listen in companionship with others, more often talking than listening. In this, there is great pleasure, even joy, and there is also great temptation. One is easily carried away in the moment and carelessly makes remarks for attention or a laugh that are based on hearsay and are derisive, defamatory or false, usually through exaggeration. To be together with others, especially in one's family, in celebration, in amusement or solace, is life-enhancing, so long as temptation is avoided, the temptation of the big mouth.

The greatest pleasure in life, I believe, is from participation in an activity, especially one that requires training, skill, physical coordination and talent. It is much more pleasurable and satisfying to be a musician than a concertgoer, to be a playwright or actor than a theatergoer, to be a game player rather than a spectator. True, our society has turned these activities of the highly trained, skilled and talented into jobs. But I still believe, even as a job, skilled performance is a pleasure for the performer greater than the pleasure of an onlooker. And this applies to those of us who are not professionals. We, all of us, will derive more pleasure from skilled activities involving physical coordination, such as swimming or playing the guitar; or expressive activities, such as writing or painting; or handy activities, such as building or repairing or just tinkering. The point is that the participant owns the skill and is not dependent on another to provide diversion or pleasure. With expertise, one gains self-sufficiency, independence, satisfaction and pride. No passive pleasure can provide so much and yet we tend to rely almost exclusively on entertainers and advertisers to provide pleasure in our lives, a debilitating and costly delusion. I think an intelligent person will resist passive pleasures and emphasize participatory and active pleasures.

Nature provides an opportunity for both. There is, of course, pleasure in viewing natural scenes in paintings or an assortment of nature magazines and calendars, all of which include astonishing photographs. It is intriguing to me that our culture expresses so much yearning and nostalgia for our roots in the countryside. Troubled characters in film and fiction go for walks beside bubbling brooks in woodsy settings. In wine and cheese advertisements, couples in love picnic among fields of wildflowers. Late-model automobiles are displayed to us as they glide glistening on two-lane country roads. It is routine to depict tenderness, happiness and consolation in natural settings, while most of us experience these emotions in traffic on the freeway. The natural beauty we actually see is largely in reproductions, paintings, calendars, nature magazines and travel brochures. Occasionally, we may enjoy the real thing from a car or train window. In any case, our pleasure from viewing nature is fleeting or subliminal. We do not pay a lot of attention to it.

There are, however, many out-of-doors activities in nature that non-urbanites are engaged in, such as farming, fishing, lumbering and construction. These are work activities and livelihood activities, and in them, the participants may actually view nature as an enemy, the inhuman, unpredictable force that can wipe out results of human efforts in a matter of minutes. To them, nature, at best, is the source of discomfort and fatigue. And yet my presumption is that these outdoor people will always prefer their lives outdoors to the lives of office and factory workers, as long as working out of doors provides a reasonable living. The open sky, fresh air, and vigorous activity are preferable to immobility in air-conditioning and artificial lighting, and subject to the demands of a machine, notably, a computer. The outdoor person is more alive.

On the other hand, not all urbanites are city-bound. Weekends they seek the outdoors. But for a large number of these escapees, nature is a challenge. The challenge is how to be in nature with all the comforts of urban life. Meeting this challenge requires inflatable mattresses, lounge chairs, insulated sleeping bags, ice chests, gas stoves, chemical toilets, music, insect repellent, thermal underwear, and purified water. It is obvious that to launch an expedition from the city into the backcountry is a sizable task of organization.

Upon arrival, the expedition must unpack and set up camp. Meanwhile, the children are happily romping about where it is open and free; the grown-ups are opening up their first beers. They too are happy for the same reasons the children are happy--open space, tall trees and fresh air. But at bedtime the people in the adjacent campsite are having a party. It is noisy, noisier in the woods at a campground than at home.

Returning home is a rerun of the preparations made for coming out, except in reverse. It is Sunday night, the traffic is heavy and the going slow. The escapees all return at once. They have had fun, the weekend was a pleasure, but only marginally because of an encounter with nature. The logistics were too demanding. Nature was hardly noticed at all.

There is still another group of urbanites, which seeks recreation in nature on weekends and vacations. They are younger than the campers, because children are not usually involved. They, like the campers, view nature as a challenge, but also they view it as an adventure. More than that, they view it as a thrill. They go skiing, cross-country biking, off-road motorcycling, hang gliding, or speedboating on a lake or river. They purchase expensive state-of-the-art equipment with which they are immensely enamored. What they do is physically demanding and they drink a great deal of water out of plastic bottles. They see nature as a challenge to endurance, speed and daring. But is it really experiencing nature?

There are also urbanites who take walks, not weekends. In most cities there are parks and miles of trails where one can walk where the natural environment is preserved. The stay-at-home walkers who walk these trails are seldom alone. They are accompanied by others with whom they engage in shoptalk. Some even carry a ghetto blaster. This form of getting outdoors and into nature surely provides fresh air and exercise and the pleasure of conviviality. But again, is this really experiencing nature?

Nature, like art and music, is most enjoyed when one has done some homework and when one knows something about what one is seeing. In fact, one does not see unless one knows what to look for or knows what one is seeing. One misses a multitude of beauty, if one only sees trees and flowers or birds and cannot see the variety among them. The woods are composed of a variety of trees with unique configurations of leaves and sometimes blossoms. Flowers in a meadow do not create just a pretty meadow. The individual flowers are of different varieties. Seeing the beauty of the individual flowers multiplies the pleasure of seeing the meadow. But seeing the individual flowers implies knowing them, knowing them by name. And so it is with birds. As an analogy, suppose you walk into a restaurant and see a roomful of diners. That is one thing. But if you know the names of most of the diners, then entering the room is an altogether different experience. Salutations are exchanged. Recognition engenders familiarity and ease and delight. In nature, it is the same, especially with birds. Knowing the names of birds means knowing their plumage patterns. A bluebird and a blue jay are quite different, in their flight patterns, foraging patterns and their calls and songs. Nature becomes a lively and enchanting place when one has done some homework and sees with knowing eyes.

While I do not deny that organized and equipped group activities in designated outdoor locations provide pleasure and, therefore, often enhance one's living experience, the pleasure derived is, to my mind, similar to that of an amusement park. It provides thrills and conviviality, but not the pleasure that nature as such provides. To truly enjoy nature one must walk alone, quietly as the Indians are said to have walked and for the same reason--not to frighten away the wildlife. When it is quiet you will hear birdsongs and birdcalls, the rustling of leaves by small animals, the snort of a deer, alert to your presence but standing still. When you walk alone, where the sky is open and the land lies open before you with patches of light and shadows reflecting the drifting clouds above, and where in the distance a mountain range lies in shades of blue, a massive against which humanity is small, and you are small and alone, you experience in this vastness and beauty the insignificance of your own affairs. Watching two crows coasting and waffling above in the thin clear air in endless time, you are truly immersed in nature, the mystery and the wonder of it. Human discourse and intercourse become irrelevant to you. And alone in nature, you find communion and eternity.

It is doubtful that animals, other than ourselves, consciously enjoy beauty. What is beauty? It is the experience of delight we enjoy when we hear certain sounds and see certain images. It is pure pleasure. It is spontaneous, although like other true pleasures, it can be cultivated. It is the highest form of pleasure. In nature, beauty is a free gift, yet most of us overlook it. It is not seen as something central to our lives. It is an incidental, not a part of the business of life. For most of us men, it is a frivolous preoccupation of the female of our species. "Look, dear, isn't that beautiful?" she says. He replies, "Yes, dear," without raising his eyes from the road ahead. Only the next destination matters and the road ahead leads to it. What else?

It occurs to me that beauty, the search for it and the creation of it, presents an intriguing rationale for living. With beauty as a major preoccupation we look for beauty everywhere and, looking, we find it everywhere. Awareness of beauty enriches our living experience. Creating beauty is fulfilling, not necessarily as an artist, but simply in our everyday living, our clothing, furnishings, and especially our gardens. Our capacity as humans to extract plants from their natural environment and replant them in gardens for the sole purpose of creating beauty is an ancient expression of the human spirit. Planting a flower garden has no pecuniary reward. It creates only beauty, but rewards the planter with awe and wonder and peace of mind. Beauty is its own reward. For contentment and well-being we need to open our hearts and eyes to beauty as it exists around us, and to the special delight derived from creating beauty in our lives.

* * *

The Importance of Place

Place is important to contentment and well-being. Finding one's place provides a sense of security and certainty. There are two aspects of place. One is the physical reality of house and home. The other is in the mind, in the imagination.

Discussing the latter first, we all have a self-image, which, as we have said, is our own perception of ourselves, based, of course, on our conjecture about how others see us. To make it even more convoluted, we project what we esteem as being what others esteem. An acquaintance of mine gave up a high-profile and high-stress job for a lower-paying and less stressful job. In her new capacity, she attended, with 30 or more others, a workshop in which each was asked to tell something about themselves. My friend told her story of her change in employment and her associates burst into applause. At the coffee break, she was the center of attention. How futile it is to find one's place on the presumed admiration of others. My friend might normally have assumed that her colleagues would have been bewildered or mystified by her rejection of a higher position and loss of esteem. She would have been dead wrong.

Employment has always involved status. Menial employment has low status, while professional employment has high status. All parents, especially immigrant parents, envision for their children professional careers. Business, the second-best choice, is a gray area, but it is where most of us find jobs. However, within business itself, there is status. Finance and banking are thought to be higher status than retail and sales. Larger is better than smaller. Microsoft has higher status than Mom's bakery. All of this, again, is in our heads. None of this is reality. Reality is what one does, day to day, hour to hour. Regardless of status, is it skillful? Is it useful? Is it satisfying? Is it congenial? Is it sustaining financially? If so, then one has found one's place in one's mind. And in one's place one is not looking around for something better. One is content with what one has.

Turning now to physical place, I have in mind one's home. It is often said that a house is not a home. We all live in houses, condominiums or apartments. Nevertheless, not everyone has found a home. Many yearn for a home. Often the missing home is the remembered home of childhood. That home was permanent and it was forever, at least until the shock of the first family move. It was intimately familiar, its sounds and smells, its latches and lights and little leaks. It was changeless, it was comfortable, it was safe. Some of us love moving to new places; others are brokenhearted to be leaving home. All of us, I believe, carry with us a remembrance of home. Of course, in the past, families lived for generations in one house, especially in agricultural communities. Few of us do today, and that loss of a physical home, a place of belonging is, I believe, at the bottom of much of our sense of lack of security. Our rootlessness and instability increase our foreboding and gnaw relentlessly at our well-being.

Is it possible to find a home today? I think it is and it is important to do so. I believe we can make a home of any dwelling, but to do so it must be endowed with permanence. By that, I mean a belief in permanence, perhaps a childlike belief. If one knows that moving is an inevitability or a probability or an aspiration, then where one lives currently will not be home, and home will remain a childhood memory. A place to stay is not a home. It is no different than a hotel room.

In one's home one will feel at home. One is familiar with its every detail, its uniqueness as one's own place. This, of course, is difficult in multiple housing. There can be no exterior uniqueness and so the uniqueness is interior. But if it is intimately experienced and is comfortable because of this intimacy, if it is maintained in an orderly and caring way, if it is pleasing upon arrival and left regretfully, if the surrounding environment is familiar, the neighbors and the storekeepers and the postman are all acquaintances and one is not about to move, then one has found a home, no matter that it is not detached housing, perhaps, because it is not. It is not one's unique home from the outside, but is certainly one's unique home from the inside.

A detached home has more uniqueness than an apartment or condominium, but not much more if it is in a modern development as it is very likely to be. Yet in contrast to an apartment or condominium, a detached house provides some ground around it, if not much, allowing one to have a connection with living things of the natural world, planting seeds in the spring and raking leaves in the fall, watching the same wrens return to the same birdhouse to raise their young each summer, experiencing the change of the seasons firsthand. One can be at home here in a more connected way, as long as one does not plan to move. Otherwise, the requirements for making any dwelling a home are the same: familiarity, identity, amenity, security and, again, permanence. For contentment and well-being, we need a place we call home.

Chapter VII

The Rudiments of Health

There is, of course, much more to living a good life. For example, one needs to be well to be happy. Among the ways we crimp, cloud, foreshorten and destroy our lives, our lack of attention to our bodies is, perhaps, the most obvious. I believe no animal has evolved which has adapted to living in a box, without physical exertion even to procure its food. Humans are no exception. Increasingly, human life is spent in confinement, in a sedentary position, with already processed food as near as the vending machine, or the refrigerator. This does not describe all human existence, since in large segments of the world there is poverty, a scarcity of food and a large proportion of the population eking out a scarce subsistence through personal endeavor.

For most of us living in the so-called developed nations, acquiring our subsistence does not require physical labor. We do not need to run to catch a chicken; we simply drive through. And this, I believe, has enormous implications for our health. Here we are living sedentary lives with an abundance of food, which requires almost no effort to obtain, yet we are living in bodies designed for vigorous exertion in obtaining food. We have the same appetite required to fuel the energy formerly required. We continue to eat food in the same quantities, if not greater quantities, than we once required for obtaining food. Our bodies react badly. Fatty flesh builds up, increasing weight that strains the heart. Fatty substances clog the arteries and overload kidneys and gallbladders, which malfunction painfully. We suffer high blood pressure, diabetes, and, ironically, a loss of energy. This is the pain I spoke of earlier.

To offset the lack of physical activity that had been demanded for survival in the past, we contrive today's substitute activities to exercise our bodies: sports and physical fitness exercises. It seems to me that these artificially contrived exercises are of utmost importance to the quality of one's life. Our bodies demand them for healthy living and longevity. Common sense tells us so. We feel exhilaration from exercise.

Again, human life differs from animal life. I have never seen a dog doing push-ups. But human intelligence tells us that we need to do push-ups. However, this intelligence creates a problem for human beings, because humans are no more inclined than other animals to do push-ups. (There is a species of lizard that I have observed which does do push-ups, and I have often wondered why.) Despite our disinclination, we do push-ups or, rather, some of us do them. What makes us do them against our inclination? A concept we discussed earlier called "will." Willpower, responding to our intelligence, makes us do them. No longer does survival requiring the search for food motivate us. We ourselves motivate ourselves. What a remarkable attribute of the human animal, the capacity to act against one's inclination! And what a tragedy it is that so many humans fail to do so!

A balance between food consumption and exercise is required for good health. This balance varies, no doubt, among individuals. How do we individually discover an appropriate balance? I would guess by body weight and energy level. We are all aware of both--if not precisely, certainly in general. We even know, most of us do, that we need to eat less and exercise more. That we do not make this adjustment when we have the capacity and intelligence to do so is, I feel, fatal, literally fatal. By fatal, I mean premature death, preceded by serious illness.

When we do adjust, the tendency is to think of dieting, changing what we eat and reducing the amount. Vigorous physical exercise is for kids and professional athletes as we sit on the sidelines and cheer. This is a mistake. As between the two, dieting or exercising, exercising is the more rewarding. Vigorous exercise is exhilarating. Dieting is not. Exercise provides a natural high, or at least a sense of well-being. Eating a balanced diet, of course, fortifies exercise, and together they provide good health. Good health is the foundation upon which a good life and a feeling of contentment and well-being are built. Nothing is more fundamental.

* * *

The Ambiguities of Work

We lead dichotomous lives. We are either pursuing work or recreation. It is often said that truly happy people are those who love their work. For most people, work is burdensome, monotonous, stressful and tiring. That is why we are paid to do it. And the reason we do it is because we are paid. We "earn" our living, the bread, clothing and shelter that maintain our lives. This is essentially the way it is. Some people find reward in work beyond monetary reward--for example, the reward of accomplishment, the reward of associated endeavor, the reward of influence and respect in or outside the work organization, and the reward of consuming beyond life's necessities--the doubtful reward of luxury. Nevertheless, I think it is not unrealistic to say that most of us spend, at minimum, one-half of our wakeful hours in occupations that are drudgery and, as we said above, sedentary. In modern industrial society, one's work is far removed from the final product, which in any case may be an intangible such as service. Work is segmented. People are trained to perform a single task at which they become proficient and efficient. In time, repeated performance of one skill becomes monotonous and dead-ended. By then work has become only a means, a means to enjoyment of one's other life--the real life, life after work. After work, one is drained. After work, there are chores, personal and household and family chores. After work we really only want to plunk down on the sofa, kick off our shoes, get a drink and a snack, and turn on some music or television. After work and after chores, we only have thoughts of recuperation and preparation for the next workday. Then it is bedtime. Our after-work life is spent.

No one has ever said that mankind needs not work for livelihood. The old saw is that there is no free lunch. And work we must. But I believe we can use judgment and our intelligence to act reasonably in the expenditure of our lifetime. How much income we really need depends upon how much we need in material goods to live a comfortable and healthy life. In truth, most of us living above the poverty level will find that we can do with less and never miss it. However, the difficulty of giving up a lifestyle and assuming another cannot be denied.

We may have achieved status, a status based on material things. Doing with less is a loss of status, status that we have worked hard to achieve and maintain. But remember our earlier thoughts. What is status? It is our perception of how others perceive us, in relation to themselves. You see others as having status, judging from their lifestyle. Then you imagine that living like them on a similar scale provides you with status in their eyes. Meanwhile, where are you in all this? You think you have gained status in the minds of others, but does that thinking give you contentment and well-being? To what extent do we live our lives to meet the regard that we imagine others will have for us, depending on our lifestyle?

I am mindful, however, that many working adults work at a minimum wage. Their income provides only for the most basic living, if that. In reality they do not have a choice as to the kind of work they do, or how much time the work consumes of their lives. Their greatest concern is finding a job and hanging on to it. If you asked such a person whether he would continue to work in his present job, given an opportunity to work at a less demanding one, the answer would be, I am sure, an emphatic no. Yet, so many of us in more-fortunate circumstances are bound as tightly to our jobs as is the poor man, believing we too must work, at all cost, to make a living. The difference is the poor man is working for a subsistence living and we, who are better off, are working for affluent living. The poor person faces true reality. We face fictitious reality. There is no real necessity for what we think we need. We are fortunate to have options. The poor person would find it incomprehensible that we ignore them.

On the other hand, the poor person, given the possibility of becoming wealthy in his present work, might well opt to continue in it. He would, I think, be making a mistake. One does not need great wealth to lead a good life. However, one does require some income. That income may be much less than one has been assuming is necessary and may be earned in ways less stressful, more congenial and healthful than the way one has been earning it. When this insight is accepted, it is often accepted with the intent to actualize it someday. Someday is a perilous speculation. A life can be lost betting on someday.

Work is largely about earning an income, although many people say they would prefer work to idleness, even if income were not the issue. Few, however, continue to work when income is not the issue and, apparently, the goal of all income earners is to reach retirement with enough money to live without working longer. But often these same income earners sabotage themselves. They spend more than they earn. They incur debt to live above their means. Debt is bondage. It is voluntary indenture. Debt does not go away. It is unforgiving. It is unrelenting. It is ruthless. Personal debt clouds one's life, hanging there, casting its shadow into the far reaches of one's mind, no matter how much one tries to forget. We can make payments now, but what if...? The intelligent person will avoid personal debt.

My discussion of work, thus far, has described work as drudgery for most of us, excepting those who have work they love. It has come to my attention that there is another approach to work that overcomes drudgery. It is the view that work is service. Most work involves commodity production. As a commodity the product is useful. If it is useful to others, then contributing to its production is a service to others. The notion of service can spill over from one's attitude toward one's job to one's attitude toward one's employer and one's fellow workers. Helping others is the opposite of helping only oneself. It changes the whole perspective from which one works. Work which was a chore becomes an opportunity; work which was drudgery becomes rewarding. Work is no longer lost time. One's life is enriched by one's work as service.

* * *

The Problem of "Ought-Tos"

We all carry a load on our backs, an invisible, intangible load. A part of this load consists of our "ought-tos," all the things we ought to do and do not do, and feel guilt because we do not do them. (Perhaps I have even added some ought-tos to your load. But if so, they are reflections of my own ought-tos.) Each day we confront our ought-tos and they hang there like clouds on an otherwise clear day. People react differently to their ought-tos. Some attack them, compulsively, determined to wipe them out by nightfall. They carry with them their daily planners and systematically abolish their ought-tos, one by one, only to confront new ought-tos the next day. Others, the group to which I belong, discover dubious priorities which command immediate attention, and necessitate delay in doing an ought-to to a more convenient time. Of course, this group to which I belong confronts the old ought-tos the next day; but they have now become a bit more onerous or difficult to do or alternatively, less urgent. We have made it thus far without doing an ought-to, so why worry? Yet it is not quite so easily dismissed. No matter how far to the rear we push an ought-to, it still blights our lives, vaguely, persistently, and reproachfully. We need to deal with our ought-tos at once to avoid the disquietude they cause us when avoided.

How can we deal with our ought-tos? I have said that I have ought-tos and am not very good in dealing with them. However, I believe two approaches can help. One has already been indicated. That is to do ought-tos promptly and consistently. Do not shirk them. (I am now imposing another ought-to, but this ought-to is important, because it relieves the burden of other ought-tos.) Although new ought-tos occur the next day, they do so without the burden of guilt that neglected ought-tos carry with them. Also, one's confidence in performing ought-tos grows, and one's sense of adequacy in living life grows as well

The second approach to the ought-tos that cloud our lives is to screen them. We should not accept all ought-tos suggested by others or thoughtlessly assumed by ourselves. We need to evaluate whether a proposed ought-to is something we can realistically do, whether it is something we want to do, whether it is something important to do, given our living reality. Is doing it something that substantially enhances our living experience, or is it simply something someone else thinks we ought to do? If we limit our ought-tos in this way, there will be many fewer ought-tos in our lives and those that remain will have our commitment. In fact, we may want to do an ought-to, in which case it is no longer an ought-to.

Not all ought-tos are alike. Those that are susceptible to closure by promptness are usually task obligations such as job demands, household and family chores, and health care. Sooner done, the better. Postponed and avoided chores exert a constant pressure, uneasiness, irritation and edginess incompatible with contentment and well-being.

But there are other ought-tos that are beyond the reach of promptness or selectivity. They are imposed externally by custom. They are the ought-tos that have become ossified by habit and consensus within one's social or ethnic or regional group. They demand wearing certain clothing on various occasions, speaking with certain intonation and mannerism, worshiping in a prescribed way, observing the rituals of season's greetings and remembering birthdays.

These ought-tos may not weigh heavily for most people, but for some they do. These are those for whom habitual customary ought-tos are meaningless and often annoying. They would prefer to ignore them and often do ignore them. Ignoring them has no serious consequence except for raised eyebrows among one's relatives and friends. There is no penalty for their neglect beyond being labeled an oddball, and perhaps that is exactly what one wants by ignoring these conventional ought-tos, especially what the young want. But then the young are not seeking contentment and well-being. Rather, they seek attention and challenge. For those of us who are older, however, it makes for peace of mind to go along with inconsequential ought-tos. They are occasional, nonessential, and only mildly disturbing. They are better done than ignored.

Finally, there are ought-tos of great importance. These cannot be ignored, postponed, or excused. Ignoring, postponing or excusing these ought-tos is detrimental to one's character and self-esteem. Foremost among these ought-tos is this: One ought to be honest, honest with others and, above all, honest with oneself, with no justifications, no alibis, no convenient fabrications. Straight on, the truth all the time. Adhering to this ought-to clears the underbrush and clutter in one's life. It simplifies life and clarifies one's relations with others. It is the cornerstone for a life of contentment and well-being. There is no compromise.

Other ought-tos of equal importance are the following. One ought to be well-wishing toward others. One ought to be modest, moderate, open-minded, flexible and empathetic. One ought to be generous and considerate. One ought to be prudent, attentive and careful. In a word, one ought to be good.

To these fundamental ought-tos we can be committed. Unlike the superficial task-oriented ought-tos that can be extinguished by action to avoid penalty, the fundamental ought-tos require sustained behavior, which is gradually and inevitably rewarded. Reason and intelligence suggest commitment to these ought-tos. They are our guidelines, the ingredients of a life of contentment and well-being.

* * *

The Clouds of Worry and Fear

Our living experience is often clouded by worry and fear. Most of our ought-tos arise out of fear, fear of the consequences of not doing something. Many of these fears are easily extinguished by timely action. Because of this easiness, we procrastinate. We know we can take care of it. It is only a matter of getting around to it. It is foolishness to allow these fears to worry us.

Fears that are more than just nagging worries are fears about future outcomes or events that we imagine might occur. We think that a danger exists. It is not now existing, but we imagine its existing and we worry that it will exist. What is more, we often imagine a danger not to ourselves, but a danger to another. We see others following what we believe are dangerous paths. We are helpless to deter them, our children or other loved ones, or even total strangers, as they, unconcerned, continue progress toward what we see as harmful misfortune. We worry in vain for the welfare of others. We are fearful for them.

I believe, as harsh as this may sound, especially to a mother, that this kind of worry blights the worrier's life and benefits the other not at all. There is very little, except death, which is inevitable in life. One's forebodings, one's convictions about the inevitability of harm to another by the persistent behavior of the other, in all probability, are chimerical. Often the foreseen never materializes and then, frequently, we the worriers chastise the subject of our worry for having caused us so much needless worry.

Of course, we also worry about ourselves as well as about others. Our personal worries are manifold. We worry that it will rain on the weekend so that we will need to cancel a planned picnic. We worry that we will not be able to pay our bills. We worry that we will make a mistake in public or that we will be late or in some other way be deficient in the eyes of others. We also worry that we will be found out in some concealment, that we will be caught. We worry that we cannot meet the expectations that others have for us or fulfill promises made. We worry about the loss of possessions, status and privileges. We worry about lost looks as we age and we worry about losing our car keys.

These worries are all needless worries. We create them by deception, by false presumptions and expectations, by dependence on others and their opinions, by exaggerating the importance of future events for oneself or mankind, and by an attitude generally pessimistic. They are mind worries.

Can we do something to alleviate this kind of worry? I believe we can. To begin with, we need to be honest with ourselves and we need to ask ourselves how much we worry for worry's sake. How much do we worry to feed our own self-importance? How much do we worry because of our own carelessness, inattentiveness, inertia and thoughtlessness? These are questions we need to continuously ask ourselves. At the same time, however, we need to do our best, without concern for the judgment of others, to appraise realistically the likelihood of adverse future events and their possible impact on ourselves or others, and we need to accept what is and what might be.

> *The man who looks for the morrow without worrying over it knows a peaceful independence and a happiness beyond all others.*
> *-- Seneca*

Worry is fear that some occurrence will or will not happen. Worry might also be thought of as fear over non-life-threatening eventualities. Fear, as distinct from worry, is a life-or-death matter.

There are those who have no fear of death, mostly the young and foolhardy. About the foolhardy, there is nothing to be said. Nor need there be. They have no fear and we are concerned here with fear. But for mature adults who have internalized the reality of death, there is fear, fear of illness, fear of accidents, and fear of bodily harm. As mature adults, we become careful and we avoid dangerous situations knowing, nevertheless, we cannot avoid death ultimately, and we fear death.

The "fear of death" is a frequently used expression, but I have never known exactly what it means. Does it mean we fear the consequences of death, a hell that awaits us, or does it mean the agony of dying?

I have already compared sleep with death. In both, we lose consciousness. We do not fear sleep. We seek it. We take pills to induce it. Drifting off to sleep is a delicious feeling. Why would dying be different? I believe at the moment of death we will want to die. Knowing this may help to ease our fear of dying. We think of dying when we do not want to die, but when we are dying we will want to. Dying, then, is nothing to fear.

> *Death is nothing to us. For what has*
> *been dispersed has no sensation.*
> *And what has no sensation is nothing*
> *to us.*
> *-- Epicurus*

There is often, however, a prolonged illness before dying and, perhaps, it is this, the agony before dying, which we fear. If so, I have two thoughts that may allay that fear. One thought is that modern medicine will ease the way with medications; the second thought is that we may have the option to determine the time of our own departure. It is not always in the hands of fate or the doctor.

However, among mature and thoughtful adults there are those who do not fear death and are not, at the same time, foolhardy. Like Socrates, they believe in the continuance of the soul. The soul leaves the body to enter a new existence everlasting from which, it is sometimes thought, the soul will eventually return to live in a new bodily form. Consequently, those who have this belief may face death without fear, but rather with curiosity and even anticipation. Obviously, belief in life after death eases the fear of death as extinction. Perhaps this is why so much faith has been placed in a life after death by humans through time immemorial.

Concerning fear, I have a confession. I have a dreadful fear of heights and precipices. I am rigid with fear on an escalator and none of my reasoning about death helps. Having fear of this kind might be a blessing. It is physical and instinctive and often saves us from injury or death. It is a survival mechanism shared by all living creatures. We cannot eliminate it from our lives, though not everyone fears being on an escalator. In fact, most do not. In more hazardous circumstances, fear may save one's life.

Finally, worry and fear will inevitably be a part of our living experience. As an intelligent person, one will be able to shed useless worry and fear, and with resignation and acceptance, deal with that which remains.

Chapter VIII

Inborn Attitudes

One's attitude toward the facts of life is also important in reducing fear and in achieving equanimity. It seems to me that humans are born with different dispositions and attitudes. They can, I believe, be changed. First, one must be aware of one's habitual attitude. Is it habitually pessimistic, doubtful, alarmist, and negative? If so, fear and discouragement will dampen one's living experience. The pitfall in such an attitude is that one becomes a victim of an enormous conspiracy of bad luck. I am not a psychotherapist, but it seems to me that those with a predisposition of looking darkly at the world around them need only remember that the world we see is our perception. It exists in our minds. It is what we think it is. There is no such thing as good luck or bad luck. Luck is a figment of our imagination. The dice fall according to the laws of probability and have no malice toward an individual gambler. When I was young, my counselor at a summer camp scolded me for bemoaning my misfortunes, saying that I failed to add up my good fortunes at the same time. Among them, of course, was the luxury of a summer camp on a pristine lake in the Adirondacks where the camp director played "Indian Love Call" on his trumpet, the notes echoing in the still evening each night at bedtime.

Others of us have an aggressive attitude. Constantly on the alert for personal grievance, we are compelled to challenge others to get our due, get our share, get recompense and get ahead. This attitude engenders a contentious and frustrating life experience. It is obvious that people with this attitude have strong desires and engulfing egos. I believe these can be modified in ways I have already discussed, especially with the magic of love.

Reject your sense of injury, and the injury itself disappears.
– Marcus Aurelius

Finally, there are others among us who are cheerful, optimistic, trusting and enthusiastic by disposition. I once looked at such persons askance. Simple-minded Pollyannas, I thought. Today, I look at them with respect. They may seem blind to a corrupt world, but their personal lives are lived with contentment and with goodwill. Since they cannot change the behavior of others, they do not blight their lives bemoaning the way others live theirs. They are born saints. They are not fearful.

* * *

Humor

Closely akin to attitude is the gift of humor. It appears to be ingrained in certain people and usually accompanying a cheerful disposition. Humor finds amusement in the ludicrous or incongruous, but this implies the wit often to convert the ordinary into humor. It also implies a level of detachment and lightheartedness that is essential to well-being. Most of all, humor with regard to oneself is an antidote to self-importance. It is not a humor that is self-deprecatory, but rather a humor that finds genuine amusement in one's own repeated foibles, awkwardness, or blunders. It is finding amusement at oneself, instead of becoming down on oneself for being imperfect. We also seek out humor in the company of others. Humor seems to be stimulated by humor even to the extent of becoming competitive, and at that point, tiresome. Humor stimulates congeniality, but can also become raucous and inconsiderate through laughter. Loud laughter does not require much wit. Good humor does. Can one develop humor? I believe so, but rather as a by-product than product of self-training. As one diminishes one's desires, overrides one's ego and becomes more loving, one will naturally become more at ease, more comfortable with oneself, and then humor and amusement will naturally emerge.

Chapter IX

God and Worship

You may have noticed an omission in my remarks, thus far, one that, perhaps, you expected to surface sooner or later. I have not mentioned God, but will do so now. I have not mentioned God, because I believe our becoming persons of maturity and goodwill is not contingent upon the worship of a god. We do not first have to go to church or, for that matter, learn to meditate or become a Yogi. We do not have to have had an enlightenment experience, although it is repeatedly reported, by those who have had such an experience, that they experience it with a sense of overwhelming love. None of these things we have to do. We simply have to start doing selfless acts. All the rest will follow. There are not even twelve steps.

Being good is inevitably connected with being religious. I suggest that we break this connection. Religious rituals may make us feel good for a while, but they do not make us people of goodwill. Religious wars, now and in the past, are shocking evidence of that. Religious groups form communities. Community meets a human need, but is not a precondition for changing oneself.

I have recently been exposed to a growing religious group which meets in a rented space on the ground floor of an office building. Members of the group gather midst happy chatter in a bare room where the metal scaffolding, supporting the roof, is exposed and painted white. At one end of the room is a low platform or stage on which are seated a drummer, a saxophonist, a bass guitarist and a pianist. At the appropriate moment, the musicians begin playing a loud rhythmic modified rock number, familiar, apparently, to the members of the congregation. They break up their chatter groups and take their places, standing in front of folding chairs, in semicircular rows, and soon everyone is singing and clapping hands and, at the appropriate moment, hugging a neighbor. Following the singing, there are announcements of upcoming events, pleas for voluntary assistance, and remarks commemorating recent birthdays. Then there is a solo singing performance with the band by an amateur rock singer with golden hair, and then the sermon. On the Sunday I attended, the topic of the sermon was "The Importance of Saving the Environment." After the sermon, there was a final sing-along about everyone being happy and, what was more, everyone happened to be happy. The congregation broke up again in new chatter groups around an outdoor buffet and then, gradually, left for home, faces aglow. Aglow with the spirit of God? Perhaps. But I believe they were aglow with fellowship, which may be the same thing.

In contrast, the cathedral of medieval Europe stresses God. The worshiper is overwhelmed by the vaulted ceilings, the marbled columns, the paintings of angels and divine patriarchs and a thunderous organ. This is power, judgment and eternity. The worshiper is made puny by comparison, a supplicant who dared to enter God's earthly sanctuary in silence to pray for forgiveness.

In the cathedral, the religious service begins with the processional. The choir and clergy, appropriately robed, enter the cathedral singing a hymn to God and with measured steps proceed, two by two, to the chancel, where they occupy pews facing one another. After reading God's word from ancient scriptures, sundry announcements are made concerning church affairs. Then the sermon. Delivered from an exalted pulpit, it is usually read from a prepared text, elaborating some principle of living, again, from God's word. In the cathedral, the sermon is barely audible to the worshipers. The service ends with the recessional and a final organ note.

The worshiper, I believe, leaves the majesty of the cathedral deeply impressed by the existence of a superhuman power, which exists in eternity, judging mortals, punishing mortals for reasons beyond human reason and rewarding others for obeying commands, which need no reasons. The worshiper leaves, believing there is a god, all just, all knowing, all seeing, who presides over life on Earth. God Almighty. This belief is a great anchor for individuals who, though uncomprehending, at least know their lives are not for naught in a random chaos. God's hand is in everything. There is design and intent in the overall, even though it is often incomprehensible in the particular to the individual. I suspect the worshiper who leaves the cathedral does not leave with a sense of community, but perhaps leaves with a sense of serenity.

I am not attempting to draw comparisons which are favorable to one form of worship as compared with another. Differences between religious forms reflect the needs and times of the worshipers who attend. Religious services are, however, essentially external occasions with elements of idolatry, imitation, conformism, distraction and self-congratulatory piety. None of this, it seems to me, has much to do with becoming a more content, well-meaning person, a good person, something we must do for ourselves by ourselves.

Forms of worship are forms of obeisance of placation, of supplication and of mortification. The forms are not God. They are in deference to God, but are not God. God is deified by worship and is made real in human form by self-proclaimed messengers of his word.

God can be conceived as a supranatural intelligence which is the creator of all existence. God, as such, is undefined--an essence within us. God is a state of mind in which God monitors us, punishes and rewards us. God is our conscience. God is, also, love and forgiveness.

God requires faith. Faith is unquestioned belief. Faith may provide meaning in one's life and an enhanced sense of contentment and well-being. But faith alone will not do. As another old saw puts it, "God helps those who help themselves."

Chapter X

Conclusion

My testament is winding down and a conclusion is at hand. I have been expressing my thoughts about living life as I approach the end of my life. I am convinced of the utility of my suggestions derived from my own experience and from my reading, which has been eclectic. They reflect no one doctrine or philosophy that I am aware of. I am not conscious of the process of formation of my thoughts and often have discovered them as I have written them. To me, they seem self-evident.

I lived half of my life dedicated to the notion that human society is perfectible. But over time, I learned that the perfectibility of society was dependent upon the agency of human beings, themselves imperfect. Disillusionment was inevitable, and gradually and reluctantly, dragging my feet all the way, I arrived at my current state of mind. We can only perfect ourselves (I use the word "perfect," meaning "improve"). Absolute perfection is, I presume, unattainable. If we are aware, or become aware, of our power to change ourselves, we can create for ourselves a good life. We cannot control others, but we can control ourselves.

We have choices. Every action is the result of choice, often habitual and thoughtless, but not necessarily so. We can train ourselves to become more thoughtful and more aware, by slowing down, by stopping to think, by remembering our guidelines. We can also understand why some choices are better for ourselves than other choices, not because of heavenly reward for our good deeds nor punishment in hell for our misdeeds, but because we understand the consequences of our thoughts and actions for our mental and physical well-being.

I do not want to get in here over my head by attempting to distinguish thought and action. A simple solution is to consider thought as action. Thought, obviously, is not always expressed overtly in words, posture, facial expression, or physical movement. Nor is overt action reflective always of thought, unfortunately. However, if we consider thought as action, although not visible, we must then say that thought can also involve choice. We can choose what we think, as well as what we do. Practitioners of meditation seek to cease all thoughts, to silence the endless chatter of the mind. If we are capable of stopping all thoughts, we certainly can stop some thoughts and, likewise, we can choose to think other thoughts. I have emphasized our freedom of choice in thought and action because, I believe, we can change ourselves. I have previously acknowledged limitations to freedom of choice, but here wish to highlight the remarkable capacity we have through choice to change our one life experience.

I have also been emphasizing the destructiveness of desire and ego to our contentment and well-being. Desire creates yearnings, cravings and expectations, none of which can ever be satisfied, because desire, momentarily fulfilled, creates new desire. The process is endless and corruptive. Likewise, the ego is never satisfied. It spawns envy, suspicion, and hurt. Ego is linked to desire, one feeding on the other. These two are the corrosives that eat away the human possibility for a good life. I have suggested that we can constrain both of these pervasive infections by becoming aware of them and in small ways, gradually, thoughtfully and persistently suppressing them in thought and action. We can do this by choosing not to act out these impulses. Habit and forgetfulness are our weaknesses and, at first, they will override our intent. But gradually we break the habit and remember our goal to maximize our life experience, a goal that cannot be achieved in the ignorance in which many pursue it.

On the other side of the coin, we as human beings have a powerful ally that does not require self-discipline. It comes naturally to us and will automatically take care of desire and egotism. That ally is love. I have gone to great lengths in defining what I believe this healing love is, this mature love. As I have said, it is not possessiveness, nor a product of desire or ego. It is not fantastical, worshipful or sexually inspired. It is a general love or, if you prefer, it is goodwill toward others. This means wishing others well, lending encouragement and help, recognizing their humanity, which is the same as our own, giving others our full attention, having patience, and avoiding hurt through gossip, ridicule or alienation. It is attributed to Jesus who said, "Thou shalt love thy neighbor as thy self." This is a command, but I believe as intelligent human beings, we can and should ask why. I also believe the answer is both obvious and ignored. The answer is that loving others makes us feel good. Yes, selflessness is selfishness. This is, perhaps, the greatest paradox of human existence.

The developed or innate characteristics of a person who is selfless, who is attentive to the needs of others, and whose own needs are satisfied with what is, is a good person. I am convinced such a person enjoys contentment and well-being. To my mind, the noblest aspiration of a human being is to become a good person. It is doable, it is rational, it is rewarding. Why not?

* * *

Afterword

In all that has been written above, my emphasis has been on the individual's search for personal well-being. The cumulative impact of the free acts of billions of individuals has not been the focus, and yet it is these acts, largely thoughtless, which threaten life on this planet today.

Also in the foregoing, I have compared, from time to time, human behavior with other animal behavior, remarking on the similarities between them. At the same time, I called attention to the enormous disparity between the large size of the human brain compared with other species. This brain has endowed the human species with the ability to alter its environment. Originally and slowly, humans converted forest to farmland, spearfishing to net trawling, walking to flight, darkness to light, cold to warmth, and hot to cool. Humans have been able, perhaps in a limited way, to turn on its head the evolutionary theory of the slow adaptation by life forms to environmental change through mutation. At present, the human species changes the environment to satisfy its desires in relatively short time. However, changes in the environment turn out to be exchanges. They are made at a cost. With a burgeoning world population and corresponding desires, the atmospheric chemical mix is being altered, the mix that gave rise to the human species. Nevertheless, millions worldwide want American freedom--the freedom of an automobile.

There is no doubt that the Earth's climate is warming. The planet has gone through warming and cooling cycles in the past over long periods of time, but presently there is evidence that humans are either creating or enhancing a new warming cycle, which is occurring in an instant of geological time. Think of it. Humans by their actions are causing a planetary environmental change. At this writing, the Arctic ice cap is breaking apart, the Alaskan permafrost is melting, and the coral reefs of the South Pacific are disappearing, their fish along with them. Nature is being turned against all life on the planet. Humans with their large brains and freedom of choice are doing this.

Is there anything we can do, you and I? Can we be content not attempting to stop the heedless onslaught of our numbers and desires? I have written above that we ought not shadow our lives by worry over matters we cannot control. We cannot individually stop a stampede of buffalo toward the precipice. However, we can reduce our desires and level of consumption. We can choose restraint. We can adhere to the guidelines above for living a good life.

I ended the discussion above by suggesting that a good person will live a good life. I am now adding the thought that becoming a good person is the best contribution an individual can make to the common well-being. We can adopt a way of life worthy of the brain and the intelligence we possess as humans, a model that will demonstrate for others a possibility for the future which is also rewarding to ourselves in our own lifetime. This we can do, but will we?

Appendix

Words of Wisdom

The quotations below, in and of themselves, provide inspiration and guidance for living a good life. Open the pages to them at any place for an occasional reminder of what living well is about.

1. He who feels punctured must once have been a bubble. (Lao Tzu)

2. Everything is but what opinion makes it, and that opinion lies within yourself. (Marcus Aurelius)

3. As a person acts so he becomes in life. (Upanishad)

4. A man is as unhappy as he has convinced himself he is. (Seneca)

5. A man who has confidence in the good things inherent in his own self, possesses all the necessities for the happy life. (Cicero)

6. It is not without good reason that we are brought to look at sleep itself for similarities with death. (Michel de Montaigne)

7. A man with outward courage dares to die, a man with inward courage dares to live. (Lao Tzu)

8. A person is made unhappy either by fear or by endless and vain desire. (Epicurus)

9. A sane man is sane in knowing what things he can spare, in not wishing what most people wish, in not reaching for things that seem rare. (Lao Tzu)

10. Ambition, covetousness, irresolution, fear and desires do not abandon us just because we have changed our landscape. (Michel de Montaigne)

11. And that, again, is how Epicurus, like the rest, reaches the conclusion we are after, that the wise man is always happy. (Cicero)

12. And since those who argue prove nothing, a sensible man does not argue. (Lao Tzu)

13. And to give myself to others without taking myself away from *me*. (Michel de Montaigne)

14. Any man who does not think that what he has is ample, is an unhappy man, even if he is the master of the whole world. (Epicurus in Seneca)

15. Anyone thinking of his own interests and seeking out friendship with this in view is making a great mistake. (Seneca)

16. As the soft yield of water cleaves obstinate stone, so to yield with life solves the insoluble. (Lao Tzu)

17. But such a life is not "normal"; it is free from sorrow, ill health, perturbation, distress of any kind. It is, in a word, total life. (Upanishad)

18. Content need never borrow, ambition wanders blind. (Lao Tzu)

19. Curb your tongue and senses and you are beyond trouble. Let them loose and you are beyond help. (Lao Tzu)

20. Death is just not being. (Seneca)

21. Death is nothing to us. For what has been dispersed has no sensation. And what has no sensation is nothing to us. (Epicurus)

22. ...desire only that to be done which is done, and for him only to gain the prize who gains the prize.... (Epictetus)

23. Everyone departs from life as if he had only just been born. (Epicurus)

24. Fail to honor people, they fail to honor you. (Lao Tzu)

25. ...fear is the anxious anticipation of distress to come. (Cicero)

26. Folly, even after it has attained what it was seeking for, is still never satisfied. But wisdom is invariably contented with what it has got. It never has anything to feel sorry about. (Cicero)

27. For me passions are as easy to avoid as hard to moderate. (Michel de Montaigne)

28. For nature does not give a man virtue: the process of becoming a good man is an art. (Seneca)

29. For the happy man, as I see him, has to be safe, secure, unconquerable, impregnable: a man whose fears are not just insignificant but notexistent. (Cicero)

30. He has all at once returned to us as a philosopher; and whence does he get this supercilious look for us? (Epictetus)

31. He therefore that would govern his actions by the laws of virtue, must regulate his thoughts by those of reason. (Samuel Johnson)

32. He who is not satisfied with a little, is satisfied with nothing. (Epicurus)

33. He whose heart is in the smallest degree set upon Goodness will dislike no one. (Confucius)

34. Honorable conduct is the most profitable: that is Providence's gift to men. (Quintilian in Michel de Montaigne)

35. How can we regulate events of which we yet know not whether they will ever happen? And why should we ever think, with painful anxiety, about that on which our thoughts can have no influence? (Samuel Johnson)

36. How easily we pass from waking to falling asleep! (Michel de Montaigne)

37. How ludicrous and outlandish is astonishment at anything that happens in life! (Marcus Aurelius)

38. How much easier it is never to get in than to get yourself out! (Michel de Montaigne)

39. I shall show you a love philtre compounded without drug or herb or witch's spell. It is this: if you wish to be loved, love. (Hecato in Seneca)

40. If it is not the right thing to do, never do it; if it is not the truth, never say it. Keep your impulses in hand. (Marcus Aurelius)

41. If terms to end a quarrel leave bad feeling, what good are they? So a sensible man takes the poor end of the bargain without quibbling. (Lao Tzu)

42. If you do not stop the start, you will never stop the race. If you cannot slam the door against

your emotions, you will never chase them out once they have got in. (Michel de Montaigne)

43. If you have assumed a character above your strength, you have both acted in this mater in an unbecoming way, and you have neglected that which you might have fulfilled. (Epictetus)

44. Illness is felt: good health, little or not at all; neither do we feel things which flatter us, compared with those which batter us. (Michel de Montaigne)

45. ...imagine yourself suddenly carried up into the clouds and looking down on the whole panorama of human activities: how the scene would excite your contempt.... Furthermore, reflect that no matter how often upborne in this way, you would still behold the same sights, in all their monotony and transience. Yet these are the things of which we make such a boast! (Marcus Aurelius)

46. In my opinion, we should lend ourselves to others but give ourselves to ourselves alone. (Michel de Montaigne)

47. In our tears we are trying to find means of proving that we feel the loss. We are not being governed by our grief but parading it. (Seneca)

48. It is better to need less than to have more. (Augustine)

49. It is impossible to live pleasantly without living prudently, well, and justly, nor is it possible to live prudently, well, and justly without living pleasantly. (Epicurus)

50. It is not without good cause that we are brought to look to sleep itself for similarities with death. (Michel de Montaigne)

51. It is our own self we have to isolate and take back into possession. (Michel de Montaigne)

52. It is reason and wisdom which take away cares, not places affording wide views over the sea. (Horace)

53. It is the mind that frees us or enslaves us. Driven by the senses we become bound; master of the senses we become free. Those who seek freedom must master their senses. (Amritabindu Upanishad)

54. Knowledge studies others, wisdom is self-known. (Lao Tzu)

55. Let me indicate here how men can prove that their words are their own: let them put their preaching into practice. (Seneca)

56. Life is consumed by procrastination, and each of us dies without providing leisure for himself. (Epicurus)

57. Like strangers in an unfamiliar country walking over a hidden treasure, day-by-day we enter the world ... while in deep sleep, but never find it, carried away by what is false. (Chandogya Upanishad)

58. Live not as though there were thousand years ahead of you. Fate is at your elbow; make

yourself good while life and power are still yours. (Marcus Aurelius)

59. Many grains of incense fall on the same alter: one sooner, another later--it makes no difference. (Marcus Aurelius)

60. My way is so simple to feel, so easy to apply, that only a few will feel it or apply it. (Lao Tzu)

61. No virtue is helped by falsehood; and the truth can never go wrong. (Michel de Montaigne)

62. Not that which goeth into the mouth defileth a man; but that which cometh out of the mouth, this defileth a man. (Jesus--Christ)

63. Nothing is sufficient for the man to whom the sufficient is too little. (Epicurus)

64. Nowadays men are so conditioned to bustle and ostentation that we have lost the feel of goodness, moderation, even-temper, steadfastness and other such quiet and unpretentious qualities.... (Michel de Montaigne)

65. Of all the things that wisdom provides for living one's entire life in happiness, the greatest by far is the possession of friendship. (Epicurus)

66. Once they have departed from reason the emotions drive themselves on; their very weakness indulges itself, venturing imprudently on to the deep and finding no place in which it can heave to. (Michel de Montaigne)

67. One becomes like that which is in one's mind-- this is the everlasting secret and most of all the courage to discover in our selves a desperately needed higher image of the human being. (Upanishad)

68. Only pursue an offender to show him the way. (Lao Tzu)

69. Our appetite scorns and passes over what it holds in its hand, so as to run after what it does not have. (Michel de Montaigne)

70. ...people's speech matches their lives. (Seneca)

71. Praise from others must follow of its own accord; our object should be our own healing. (Epicurus)

72. Reject your sense of injury and the injury itself disappears. (Marcus Aurelius)

73. Seek not that the things which happen should happen as you wish; but wish the things which happen to be as they are, and you will have a tranquil flow of life. (Epictetus)

74. Straightforwardness and simplicity are in keeping with goodness. (Seneca)

75. The gift is to the giver and comes back most to him--it cannot fail. (Gotama--Buddha)

76. The greatest fruit of self-sufficiency is freedom. (Epicurus)

77. The greatest thing in the world is to know how to live to yourself. (Michel de Montaigne)

78. The infancies of all things are feeble and weak. We must keep our eyes open at their beginnings; you cannot find the danger then because it is so small: once it has grown, you cannot find the cure. (Michel de Montaigne)

79. The invincible shield of caring is a weapon from the sky against being dead. (Lao Tzu)

80. The key to understanding another is within oneself. (Anonymous)

81. The life of folly is empty of gratitude, full of anxiety: it is focused wholly on the future. (Maxim from Greece in Seneca)

82. The passion of love is a craving from which good men are free. (Zeno in Diogenes Laertius)

83. The people who run hardest after pleasure are the least likely to catch what they are after. (Cicero)

84. The place one's in, though, doesn't make any contribution to peace of mind: it's the spirit

that makes everything agreeable to oneself. (Seneca)

85. The tranquil man is not troublesome to himself or to another. (Epicurus)

86. The whole universe is change, and life itself is but what you deem it. (Marcus Aurelius)

87. The wise man neither rejects life nor fears not living. (Epicurus)

88. The wise men teach us well to save ourselves from treacherous appetite and to distinguish true and wholesome pleasures from pleasure diluted and crisscrossed by pain. (Michel de Montaigne)

89. There is enough in the world for everyone's need; there is not enough for everyone's greed. (Isha Upanishad)

90. There is no need to run outside for better seeing…. (Lao Tzu)

91. There is no point in getting angry against events: they are indifferent to our wrath. (Plutarch)

92. They lacked the cardinal virtues of justice, moral insight, self-control and courage. (Seneca)

93. Those who know do not tell. Those who tell do not know. (Lao Tzu)

94. To know yourself and not show yourself, to think well of yourself and not tell of yourself, be that your no and your yes. (Lao Tzu)

95. To the very last no one ever saw Socrates in any particular mood of gaiety or depression. Through all the ups and downs of fortune his was a level temperament. (Seneca)

96. True living would take from those with too much enough for those with too little, whereas man extracts from those with too little still more for those with too much. (Lao Tzu)

97. Very soon you will be dead; but even yet you are not single-minded, nor above disquiet, not yet unapprehensive of harm from without, not yet

charitable to all men, nor persuaded that to do justly is the only wisdom. (Marcus Aurelius)

98. Walking in silence through the healthy woods, pondering questions worthy of the wise and good. (Horace)

99. What difference does it make, after all, what your position in life is if you dislike it yourself? (Seneca)

100. We can never control well any business which obsesses and controls us. (Michel de Montaigne)

101. We do not go: we are borne along like things afloat, now bobbing now lashing about as the waters are angry or serene. (Michel de Montaigne)

102. What could be more foolish than a man's being afraid of people's words? (Seneca)

103. When measured by a natural purpose of life, poverty is great wealth, limitless wealth, great poverty. (Epicurus)

104. Where you arrive does not matter so much as what sort of a person you are when you arrive there. (Seneca)

105. Whereas moral goodness, according to my interpretation, is essentially something free and undefeated: the whole point of morality is its independence. (Cicero)

106. Which means more to you, you or your renown? Which brings more to you, you or what you own? (Lao Tzu)

107. Why do we go against nature's laws and make our happiness a slave in the power of others? (Michel de Montaigne)

108. Yield and you need not break: bent you can straighten. (Lao Tzu)

109. You ask what is the proper limit to a person's wealth? First, having what is essential, and second, having what is enough. (Seneca)

110. You ought to do nothing in your life that will make you afraid if it becomes known to your neighbor. (Epicurus)

111. You should live for the other person, if you wish to live for yourself. (Seneca)

112. Your face will cease to be its present picture of sadness as soon as you take your eyes off yourself. (Seneca)

113. This is the sort of person a truly wise man needs to be. He will never do anything he might regret--or anything he does not want to do. Every action he performs will always be dignified, consistent, serious, upright. He will not succumb to the belief that this or that future event is predestined to happen; and no event, therefore, will cause him surprise or strike him as unexpected or strange. What ever comes up, he will continue to apply his own standards; and when he has made a decision, he will abide by it. A happier condition than that I am unable to conceive. (Cicero)

Who is Who

The quotations above stand on their own for their wisdom. The name of the person who voiced them, originally, does not add or detract from the inherent value of the words. But it is of tremendous interest, I believe, that people living 2500 years ago, as with the Upanishads and others living later throughout antiquity, knew so much about how to live life. They knew more, perhaps, than we do today. Their standard of living was primitive as compared with ours. Their minds were not.

Upanishads (800-400 B.C.) are spiritual treatises having similar importance for the Hindus as the bible has for Christians. They are not the work of a single person.

Lao Tzu is said to have been born in 604 B.C. His "Way of Life," as recorded by his followers, is the basis for Taoism, one of the world's great religions.

Guatama (563-483 B.C.) was a wandering teacher, founder of a monastic order and, perhaps unintentionally, founder of a religion. Commonly referred to as Buddha.

Confucius (551-479 B.C.) was a teacher, philosopher, and political theorist. His ideas have influenced all of Asia. He taught the "way of goodness."

Epicurus (341-271 B.C.) established one of the most famous and, today misunderstood, philosophical schools of antiquity.

Zeno (335-263 B.C.) was founder of the Stoic school of philosophy from which, it is believed, much of the Christian doctrine was derived after Jesus.

Cicero (106-43 B.C.) was a Roman orator and statesman. He wrote extensively about moral and political philosophy and on religion.

Horace (65-8 B.C.) was a Roman lyric poet and satirist.

Seneca (4 B.C.-65 A.D.) was a Roman minister under Nero. He was also an essayist, dramatist and the author of "Letters from a Stoic," from which the quotations above have been drawn.

Quintilian (35-96 A.D.) was a lawyer and a teacher of rhetoric. He taught that an orator (lawyer) must be a good citizen and, therefore, virtuous.

Epictetus (55-135 A.D) was born a slave, but was freed later in life. He taught philosophy in Rome until philosophers were banned from Rome. He then migrated to Greece, where, through his teaching, he sought to transform Stoicism into a way of life.

Diogenes Laertius (3rd century B.C.) was an Epicurian philosopher best known, today, for his work "On the Lives, Opinions and Sayings of the Philosophers."

Saint Augustine (354-430 A.D.) became a bishop and was a voluminous writer on theology and philosophy. He is best known for his "Confessions."

Thomas A. Kempis (1380-1471 A.D.) was the author of "The Imitation of Christ," a book which has had a profound influence among Christians for over 500 years.

Michel de Montaigne (1533-1592) was the author of "The Essays," a record of his personal thoughts. The Penguin Press (1991) edition is 1283 pages in length.

Samuel Johnson (1709-1784 A.D.) was an outstanding literary figure of the 18th century. The quotations above are taken from a series of essays, each separately published as the "Rambler."

The End

About the Author

Leigh Rhett has served in various capacities, throughout his career, as a college and university administrator. He retired after ten years as President of the University for Humanistic Studies in San Diego, California. He holds a Law Degree from University of Virginia, a Master's degree from Columbia University, and a Ph.D. from New York University. His fields of interest are in political economy, environmental issues and in philosophy. He is a devoted photographer of nature at hand, especially, wild flowers.

Dr. Rhett lives with his wife and good friend, Alice Zheng, Ph.D., in Halifax County in rural Virginia.